The Rules of Rebellion

The Rules of Rebellion

Child Abductions in Paris in 1750

Arlette Farge and Jacques Revel

Translated by Claudia Miéville

Polity Press

English translation © Polity Press 1991
First published as *Logiques de la foule*
Copyright © Hachette, Paris, 1988

This translation first published 1991 by Polity Press
in association with Basil Blackwell

Editorial office:
Polity Press, 65 Bridge Street,
Cambridge CB2 1UR, UK

Marketing and production:
Basil Blackwell Ltd
108 Cowley Road, Oxford OX4 1JF, UK

ISBN 0 7456 0731 4

British Library Cataloguing in Publication Data
A CIP catalogue record for this book is available from the British Library.

Typeset in 12 on 14 pt Bembo
by Acorn Bookwork, Salisbury, Wilts
Printed in Great Britain by Billing and Sons Ltd, Worcester

Contents

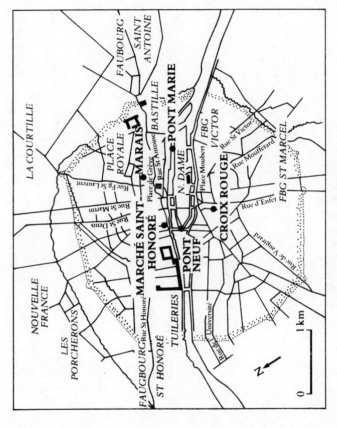

Areas of the Revolt of 1750

Introduction

Is it cruel or is it kind? We often speak about a town in the same way we speak of a person. We observe its moods, describe its temperament and imbue it with a personality of its own. We study the town as we would study an unpredictable child. We scrutinize its enigmatic form as though it were a woman. We watch it living and breathing, hoping to discover its secret.

For a long time, the lucid yet inscrutable spirit of Paris has been meticulously examined. In the eighteenth century, however, this ceaseless commentary on the town begins to change in content and function and aims to become useful as applied knowledge. It is then that the urban area becomes the subject of precise study and experimentation. Administrators, doctors and politicians all try to master the city's secrets in order to organize it more efficiently. Any disturbing sentiments of uncertainty are relegated to mere chroniclers and bystanders. In spite of this, Paris resists the confidence of the experts, disconcerts their certainties and evades their classifications and generalizations. Sooner or later they too must confront those mysteries which they had believed to be soluble: the town, the people, the crowd.

The capital had a good reputation on the whole. Louis Sébastien Mercier, who spent a lifetime as chronicler of Paris, notes in his *Tableau de Paris* (1782) that the city was generally 'peaceful' and his opinion was widely shared in the Age of Enlightenment. Diarists and journalists agree in acknowledging that the people of Paris are 'by nature good, docile and far removed from any hint of turmoil.'[1] This calm nature does not, however, signify apathy. Mercier – who, probably mistakenly, denies the Parisians any political consciousness – is aware of the signs and gestures by which, day by day, they establish a common identity: 'They use slapstick to rebuff the cannons or they shackle the Royal power with witticisms. They punish the monarch by their silence or else pardon him with applause. They will withhold "Long Live the King" if they are displeased or they will reward him with their cheers. The people of the Halles have an unerring instinct in these matters.'[2] However, this lively state of balance is not always maintained. Those who devote themselves to observing and predicting the city's reactions are often confounded by the city itself. They list its caprices, its sulks and, occasionally, its rages. They know that beneath this great tranquil body there also lie disturbing hidden forces.

Is it cruel or is it kind? It only needs a trifle to tip the scales and for the peaceful surface to crumble. It could be a bread shortage, fire or flood, fear and rumour running through the streets, a festivity or a fight. Then the shadows deepen, the highlights become sharply accentuated, and Paris totally defies description. At such moments the town emerges for what it really is: a saturated space, a tangled web of human beings, embedded but constantly shifting and elusive. Then one no longer speaks of Parisians but of the crowd, the 'populace' which seizes the streets to wreak its own havoc.

Here we will attempt to relate the events of one such episode. It is the story of a revolt which, true to the nature of all such reports, is made up partly of open talk and partly of secrets. In 1750 the people of Paris rose up against their rulers and the police and accused them of abducting their children, who were disappearing without trace. The accusation was shocking and extremely serious. It was also unique and almost bizarre, which is doubtless why the episode has interested many historians before us.[3] The story serves to remind us that the century which heralded the triumph of reason also nurtured the Saint-Médard convulsionnaries, the search for the philosopher's stone and the spread of mesmerism's wonders. This was the era for all kinds of explorations and spiritual journeys. On another level, however, this uprising can also be seen as an expression of the ambiguous everyday relationship existing between the people and public authority. Behind its dramatic movements, the revolt reveals a set of beliefs, values, actions and relationships arising from the experience of ordinary daily life. The episode was unique but, at the same time, mundane.

The town of Paris presents a blurred image and the uprising adds an element of confusion which complicates the picture still further. Nevertheless, we have chosen to study the events from the texts which relate them, and by the closest possible examination of the archives, which still tell us the story of a revolt. We do not expect to gain any additional reality from this chosen form of myopia, nor a greater closeness to the story's protagonists. On the contrary, we hoped to achieve a certain sense of displacement by adopting this approach. Conversely, at other times, we have chosen the more distant view in order properly to place the event in the series which gives it greatest significance. These two approaches, both of which involve a series of different variations of scale, work in opposite directions. They reveal different frameworks and highlight different areas but are, nevertheless, complementary. The second approach seeks to establish a context in which the rebellion can be placed and fully examined. The first, on the other hand, focuses on those mysterious elements which form part of all such stories, elements which resist generalization and typology and are perhaps ultimately incomprehensible. We wanted to acknowledge this unknown quantity to which the sources kept drawing us back; we did not want to be intimidated by it but wished rather to use it to our advantage in an attempt to grasp the essence of that, to us, most disquieting phenomenon, the rationale of a crowd in the grip of fear and anger.

From the confusion of evidence that makes up this fragmented, elusive story we have tried to capture actions and manifestations at their very moment of inception, when the field of possibilities is still wide open and before any fixed significance has become ascribed to them. Even before establishing a comprehensive interpretation of the episode, these seemingly random actions suggest that a scenario of conflict already existed. All involved in the events act out their particular roles as though they are simply improvising on a very familiar situation. We hoped to reveal the normal social framework, its values and its marks of recognition, all of

which may be discerned through the exaggerated cries
and gestures of the uprising. There is no doubt that the
revolt acts as a magnifying glass, enlarging and distorting the picture of ordinary everyday life. Nevertheless,
the characters in the story are instinctively able to weave
their own inventions into the common pattern that
gives them form and significance. We have attempted to
distinguish the outlines of prevalent social assumptions
beyond the logical processes at work in this rebellion.

The Landscape of Revolt

In May 1750 Paris was in a state of fever. Once again the town had become affected by the number of its poor. For several months the chroniclers had been recording the daily mounting tension in the city. Two years earlier, in 1747–8, famine had again struck throughout certain regions of the kingdom, driving onto the highways the usual stream of starving vagrants, many of whom ended up in the capital. What did they hope to find there? Probably nothing specific: some crumbs of the capital's wealth, a job, a lucky break or perhaps simply contact with other people living, like themselves, on the edge. However, their very presence was burdensome enough to provoke anxiety and disapproval: 'Tramps, layabouts, rascals and other vagabonds . . . are congregating in public places, on the embankments and in other parts of town to play cards or ball games. Some of them play the stick game, smashing windows and street lights.'[1] Underlying the inactivity and mischievous games of the idle, it was really their dangerous gregariousness that provoked such disapproval. These disreputable types were occupying space in Paris to which they had no right.

The problem was not new, nor were the solutions proposed by the authorities. Since the end of the Middle Ages, an impressive arsenal of repressive measures had been in existence and had been employed to the full in times of crisis. New powers had been added to these, which allowed the police to clear the streets of vagrants by charging and imprisoning them and even sometimes putting them to compulsory work. The royal edict of 1749 added nothing new to these established sanctions. Equally established was the antagonism felt by the people of Paris towards interference by the archers[2] and exempts (constables)*. Their actions invariably led to skirmishes when the crowds sided with the vagrants and came to their aid. Between December 1749 and April 1750, the repressive measures deployed seem to have been enforced with particular rigour. These were matched by the Parisians' no less decisive response and during those five months, fifteen 'violent eruptions' occurred with increasing frequency.[3] A rumour began to spread through the town that the police were not only arresting vagrants, but that children, too, had disappeared, and that some parents had had to pay a ransom for them. At this point the rumour was still so faint that the contemporary diarists paid it little attention, although they were ever alert to the daily catalogue of ills in the city. The affair was not yet interesting. It became so, abruptly, in the month of May 1750.

On 1 May, in the Faubourg Saint-Laurent, a group of about twenty young people were playing beside the gutters. Faithful to his instructions, Sébastien le Blanc, constable of the Watch, arrested six of them 'to make an

---

*Exempt: this was the term used during the Ancien Régime for the lowest ranking police officers and has been translated as 'constable'.

example of them'. The children were between 13 and 15 years old. As soon as people began to realize what was happening, the whole neighbourhood became alarmed. The incident was witnessed by some soldiers of the *gardes françaises*,[4] who regarded it as serious enough to step in and oppose the arrest. Swords were drawn. There was some jostling, some confusion, a few injuries. However, the officers of the Watch managed to load the children on a wagon, which took them to the Châtelet prison. The skirmishes between the police and the soldiers multiplied during the next few hours and in fact the clashes must have gone on for several days. On 16 May, the lawyer Barbier finally noted in his diary:

> For a week now people have been saying that police constables in disguise are roaming around various quarters of Paris, abducting children, boys and girls from five or six years old to ten or more, and loading them into carriages which they have ready waiting nearby. These are the children of working families and others who are allowed out and about in the neighbourhood either running errands or going to church. Since the constables wear civilian clothes and since they visit different areas, the business did not make much of a stir at first.[5]

On the same day, the eve of Pentecost, one of those carriages was going along the rue des Nonnains d'Hyères. The vehicle was full of archers with a constable in charge and they did not pass by unnoticed. 'A woman holding a child by the hand . . . cried out that these rascals were only looking for a chance to abduct people's children. This led to a riot on the spot and, all the ordinary folk of the district having joined in, they fell upon the archers and treated them with the utmost cruelty.[6] In fact the archers were forced to seek refuge in the residence of Commissioner de Rochebrune where the Watch had come and released them to safety. The episode left one dead and several injured. The important point was that the incident had involved the whole district from the Marais to the Temple and was a clear expression of people's frustration. Anything to do with the police was liable to unleash fear and anger. One of the archers, who had hidden in a beer merchant's shop, overheard the mutterings of the women searching for him: ' "One of them's still here, the dog. We'll get him! He must die." When he appeared they shouted, "There he is!" and tried to attack him.'

Suspicion was liable to fall on anyone, at any moment. The following day two peaceful passers-by were seized by the crowd and beaten up at Les Porcherons. Their only crime was that of being strangers in the neighbourhood.

That evening, everything was poised to erupt into a very serious situation and yet still nothing was ignited. The whole town was afraid but people were still busy arming themselves against the kidnappers. Posters appeared on the walls, placed by schoolmasters warning families to be vigilant: 'Parents are warned not to allow their children to go to school alone but to accompany them and collect them for we can take no responsibility for the consequences.'[7] The acolyte who taught the children of the poor in the parish of Saint-Gervais had only twelve of the eighty-five pupils he normally expected each day, and those twelve were 'shaking with fear'. Here and there people organized themselves. Forty years later the glazier Ménétra still remembered that his father came to fetch him from school 'with seven strong cooper lads each carrying a crowbar over his shoulder'.[8] Everyone had a story to tell and Paris was all ears.

It was into this atmosphere of fear and suspicion that the revolt truly exploded on 22 and 23 May. It did not erupt in one place but in various scattered areas of the city, ordinary districts where people lived and worked. The locations are probably not significant in themselves; they were contingent on random minor incidents such as a child who thought he or she was being followed, a police spy being recognized, the passage of the Watch. Violence was ready to erupt everywhere at the slightest provocation. Clashes between the people and the forces of order happened abruptly like flashes of temper. The town flared up sporadically in intermittent bursts without ever breaking out into total rebellion.

On 22 May, six serious confrontations shattered six different quarters of Paris. There was no point of contact between them but in each separate district, on both sides of the river, the scenario was more or less identical. The only variables were the size of the crowd and the gravity of the events. From morning till night these districts erupted in turn: St Jean-de-Latran cloisters, the Faubourg Saint-Denis, the rue du Gros-Chenêt, in the Marais, the porte Saint-Martin district, the carrefour de la Croix-Rouge on the Left Bank and finally, the Pont Neuf.

The beginning was always the same: a street scene interpreted instantaneously and collectively. In one case, a disabled veteran from Les Invalides who had celebrated his leave by getting drunk, forced a street musician to play the hurdy-gurdy outside the collège des

Quatre-Nations. That was enough for some to cry, 'He's no soldier, he's one of those constable rascals in disguise come to kidnap the children!'[9] The crowd of onlookers, who had been amused by the soldier's antics up to that point, then hurled themselves at him intending to lynch him. The only safety lay in flight. In all these confrontations people were prepared to down tools instantly at the sound of the very first shout. Servants were summoned to windows and urged to come down and join the chase and the whole street was immediately given over to the hunt. If a 'thief' was caught, he was at once attacked with fists, sticks or stones. The fugitive had only one chance, to reach a place of safety: this usually meant a police commissioner's residence. Even if he succeeded in this, he was still not home and dry because his pursuers would then lay siege to the house and demand that he be delivered to them. Occasionally, as happened at the Faubourg Saint-Denis and the Porte Saint-Martin, an officer of the Watch managed to restore calm by reasoning with the rioters. More often, however, violence prevailed. The crowds which, according to the police, sometimes numbered four or five thousand people, broke windows, forced doors down, stoned public buildings and ransacked local shops for weapons to fight with. Naturally, there was also some looting but in only one case did matters go further. Several dozen young people left the fighting in the rue de la Calandre at the Pont Neuf and tried unsuccessfully to break into the armourers' shops on the Pont Saint-Michel. One witness was later to confirm that the youths were shouting 'that they needed guns immediately to kill those villains'.[10] The rioters were slow to disperse and peace had still not returned to Paris by 3 o'clock the next morning.

The revolt flared up again early the following day, Saturday 23 May, the eve of the feast of the Holy Trinity. This time events were concentrated in one district of the Right Bank encompassing the parish of Saint-Roch between the Saint-Honoré market and the Palais-Royal. The revolt lasted all day and with increasing violence. The police archives and legal documents deal with the events as they occurred and consequently we know very little about the initial incident that set them in motion. It would seem that a constable called Labbé tried to take an eleven-year-old child from the Pont Marie. The scene was witnessed by a drummer of the *gardes françaises* who raised the alarm. A crowd immediately rushed to the scene and freed the child, while the officers of the Watch managed to escape. But for Labbé it was the beginning of a long protracted chase which ended that evening in his murder.

He led his pursuers towards the Saint-Honoré market, his home ground; here he hoped to find protection. It was a bad move. He was recognized and followed almost immediately. Labbé managed to escape the rioters twice before finally being cornered in an attic room where he had hidden under the bed. The Watch arrived on the scene just in time to save him from being lynched and he was taken to the nearby residence of Commissioner de la Vergée where a statement of the arrest was to be prepared. But the crowd were not satisfied and the scene turned to confusion. Some time later, before the examining magistrate, the Commissioner gave his own version of the extremely tense situation, which he described in bureaucratic prose:

. . . Having descended to our study, we then asked the populace who had gained entry what the matter concerned. We were informed that this individual had that morning arrested a certain woman's child. Therefore, after having told the officers of the Watch to leave the study door open, we asked if anyone knew the woman concerned, whereupon several persons replied that someone had gone to fetch her. We answered in such a way as to be clearly heard by a large crowd in these words, 'My friends, I will deliver justice and commit this individual to prison.' They appeared to be satisfied with this and nothing untoward was said or done in our house or courtyard. As we had seen an agitated crowd from our window and as we had but ten officers of the Watch present, we told one or two of the said officers, including the sergeant, to relay to the people in the street our intention to commit the individual to prison. However the sergeant reported back almost immediately that the populace in the street would not listen and wanted only to kill the individual who had been brought before us, and, having understood that they were powerless, the officers of the Watch closed the carriage gates, which the crowd then set themselves to break down. Several of those who had brought the individual before us then bade us go up to our living quarters saying that they would be sorry if any mishap were to befall us, which would certainly be the case should the populace succeed in forcing an entry. From our apartments we saw that the crowd had broken down the carriage gates as well as those of the wine merchant next door, which gave access from the street to our courtyard into which they were now throwing stones. The Watch were holding the people at bay by pointing their bayonets at them and seeing that they were thus prevented from entering, someone in the crowd fired two shots from beneath the gates. The Watch fired one shot, a third shot came from the crowd, then the officers fired two more shots, which succeeded in scattering the crowd and diffusing their violence. The officers of the Watch had taken the man into our study prior to escorting him to prison when the crowd frenziedly tore him from their hands, whereupon the small group of officers, perceiving that they were helpless and believing their lives to be in danger, withdrew to one side. We heard later that the individual tore himself away from the crowd but was recaptured in the rue Saint-Roch where he was beaten and stoned to death . . .[11]

The murder of Labbé did not, however, mark the end of collective vengeance. His corpse was dragged before Lieutenant General Berryer's house. Berryer was the man responsible for the police in Paris and the King had charged him with the task of ridding the city of vagrants. The crowd were preparing to carry out another siege but the magistrate eluded them by escaping through his garden. At that point brigades of the Watch arrived in force and this persuaded the rioters to abandon their plan. But they were still not satisfied. That evening, when the archers carried the victim's body to the morgue on a ladder, the crowd followed them all the way in watchful, mocking silence.

At the end of this day of violence, the authorities seem at last to have realized the gravity of the situation. At Versailles the duc de Luynes, assiduous chronicler of the minutiae of court life, records the event – almost reluctantly – between the intrigues of the clergy and accounts of the King's hunting: 'There have also been several uprisings in Paris over the last few days . . .'.[12] The chroniclers thus began to treat the events more seriously.[13] Within the space of two days the matter had become urgent. The Government was anxious and could no longer treat the affair as a matter purely for the police.

However, Paris was surprisingly calm on Sunday 24 May. Sightseers went to walk around the scenes of the uprising, the presence of the Watch not being enough to dampen their curiosity. It was no longer a time for overt violence. But that evening, towards 10 o'clock, a small group of people gathered in the rue Bout du Monde under the windows of the laundress Lorrain's house. She had been Labbé's mistress and he had lived there with her. As a reminder perhaps that the murdered constable had been denied the last sacraments, a derisive form of liturgy was enacted in the street. By the light of a wood fire, they slit a cat's throat; then followed a travesty of religious ceremonial. The animal was 'blessed' with water from the gutter, the *De Profundis* and *Libera Nos* were sung, and the carcass was thrown into the flames amidst jeers and threats against all police spies who could well 'end up like this cat'.[14]

There followed a kind of post-battle lull during which a tally was taken of those dead and injured in the events of May. Partisans on both sides began to blame the work of agitators for the troubles. The police set to work to compile a dossier and were soon referring to 'a group of bandits formed with the express intention of whipping up the people'. There were mutterings everywhere in town against police inspectors and their spies and some names began to be mentioned. The abduction rumour was still strongly prevalent, in fact it even reached the suburbs: Vincennes, Bagnolet, Vitry and Saint-Cloud where, according to Inspector Roussel, 'far from fading out, these seditious rumours are, rather, on the increase'.[15]

Matters remained unsettled. On 24 May the Lieutenant General of Police, the King's Lawyer and the First President of Parliament held a meeting in an attempt to restore calm. They had very little room for manœuvre since they had to deal with the effects of the disturbances and their putative causes at one and the same time. The day after the meeting, Parliament issued a ruling which amply demonstrates the inherent ambiguities of the affair.[16] One of its members, councillor Sévert, was charged with conducting a three-fold enquiry. His brief was to inquire into the revolt itself and where the responsibility for its violence lay; into 'those who had spread false rumours about orders to abduct children and were consequently responsible for the various emotions arising from this rumour'; finally, and almost incidentally, to inquire into the possible existence of kidnappers. Also a series of public-order measures were issued that were designed to restore calm to the capital.[17]

This document was equivocal to say the least, since it attempted to deal with a malicious rumour while at the same time presupposing an underlying truth to the story. Parliament's ruling had necessarily to be a wide one, because it had to meet the contradictory expectations and anxieties of both the authorities and the people of Paris before opening the way to the judicial process. The evidence which was gathered together from that point until the beginning of July involved not only those directly implicated in the events or their aftermath but a whole network of other witnesses including anxious parents and children. This mass of evidence provides the bulk of the information available to us today about the whole affair.[18]

Fragments of Revolt

Here then is an account of the Paris uprising of 1750 to add to those accounts already in existence.[19] The story can be simplified or embellished with fresh detail at will. This account is honest and verifiable against the sources; yet it is necessarily deceptive since the very nature of such an account introduces an element of order and coherence to the fragmented events of the actual revolt. Working from a chronological framework inevitably implies a narrative order, a chain of events which appear to fall into a logical pattern with a beginning and an end. No matter how minimally this seeming order is imposed in the telling of the story, it is actually profoundly alien to the true experience of those days in May 1750. The real protagonists of the events had the usual myopic vision of those closely involved in a battle or rebellion and saw very little beyond their immediate surroundings. The most serious problem is that by its very nature the true tale of the rebellion cannot adequately be told. It is easy enough to imbue the events with meaning; in fact various interpretations were suggested at a very early stage. But those incidents, which rose like bubbles in a pond to disturb the calm surface of Paris, have always defied effective description.

Indeed some contemporary reporters saw no necessity for detail. The *Amsterdam Gazette* of 29 May laconically informed its readers of the events in Paris. Nothing in this brief report indicates the true scope of the revolt and details were clearly perceived as unimportant. The political lesson to be drawn had already overtaken the events themselves:

Paris, 25 May 1750
The King, having returned from Choisy on Friday, is back today and will spend three days there. The Queen has entirely recovered from the cold which has indisposed her for some days.

Paris, 29 May 1750
The public uprisings which have been taking place in various parts of the capital were caused by false rumours spread by malicious individuals bent on disturbing the public peace by asserting that some people had been ordered to kidnap children. These riots lasted until the 23rd of this month when the First President went to Versailles for an extraordinary Council meeting, which was held in the presence of the King. On the 25th, Parliament being then assembled, the Court issued the following ordinance: [the text of the ordinance is then quoted in full].

The King, who went to Choisy on the 24th, is returning to Versailles to take part in the procession of the feast of the Holy Sacrament.

The *Amsterdam Gazette* account stresses the maintenance of order. It retains no fact or circumstance of the uprising itself but only the imputation which justified the legal action to be taken by Parliament. On 2 June, the *Mercure Historique et Politique*, which was published in Paris by people close to the authorities, gave an apparently quite different version of the story. Under the customary fictional guise of a correspondence, the account of events was able to be more informative.

Public attention in this town has recently been focused on an uprising the cause of which was negligible but which could have led to disastrous results had measures not immediately been taken to suppress it. The cruel, reckless manner in which police constables were abducting children from the streets for no apparent reason provoked a riot near the Pont-Marie which spread like lightning to the rue Saint-Antoine. From these two busy, populated areas the uprising then spread into adjacent streets and soon practically the whole town was involved. As people are all too ready to commit appalling excesses on such occasions, the least of which is looting, law-abiding local inhabitants closed their shops and houses and stayed at home. Twenty squadrons of the Watch, both foot and horse, were unable to disperse the rebellious crowd without resorting to ultimate sanctions. They were forced to open fire; one man was killed and a dozen were wounded. The riot then began to be quelled, a process which was finally achieved by the approach of nightfall and the doubling of patrols. The matter was taken up by Parliament and at the King's Council.

The report is perfunctory and biased but it has all the hallmarks of exemplary tales chronicling the marvels and miseries of the times that frequently appeared in pedlars' leaflets and pamphlets: a handful of 'true' facts, stories of police oppression, a recognizable locality, details of dubious information used to put flesh on the bones of what could basically be an account of any uprising, anywhere. The correspondence in the *Mercure* does not state what actually took place but sketches a general image of rebellion, then adds a few extraneous details for verisimilitude. And why would anyone want to know more? What could they learn? The journalist concludes casually, 'Some ordinances and decrees were issued concerning the uprising but I will not give you details of these or of subsequent events unless you have a great desire for further information, in which case you must let me know.'

The newspapers were in a hurry. Also, they were often controlled, at least indirectly, by the political powers and in fact many newspapers omitted to report the events at all. We can also look for information at the other end of the spectrum, at grass-roots level. The aim of the judicial inquiry, under the direction of Parliament, was to elicit straightforward accounts from all those people positively identified as having been present at the scene of the troubles. This information provides another version of events. It is a piecemeal account subject to interruptions by witnesses and the direction of the examining magistrate's questions. Furthermore, it is particularly fragmented because it is mainly composed of snatches of information gleaned from individual accounts whose plethora of detail aimed to confuse rather than clarify.

The witnesses took care whenever possible to dissociate themselves from the events. Adrienne Boucher, a fishmonger, was at the Quinze-Vingts market on 23 May and did not deny having witnessed 'the brawl'. She admitted to having seen Labbé, whom she did not identify, appear with 'his face covered in blood wearing a red jacket or suit. He escaped down an alley-way beyond the butcher's shop . . . the people chasing him surged into the market place, which was very crowded.' The details are precise, the scene has the ring of truth. But as soon as the magistrate asked his next question, 'What happened to the man?' she appeared not to have seen anything, which is plausible, nor to have known anything about it, which is less so. She simply chose not to say any more. 'She did not see him come out of the house because she was too busy getting on with her trade in safety.'[20] This same, evasive tactic was used by Claude-Joseph Frizon, a young apprentice, who witnessed glimpses of Labbé's death scene. He certainly saw that Labbé was being attacked but 'it horrified him too much' so he went on his way returning 'not long after the man was dead and he saw the corpse being dragged to Monsieur Berryer's house'.[21]

It was a simple ploy; the less one had seen, the less one was involved. Joseph Jacquet, a coachman accused of having joined in the disturbance in front of Commissioner de Rochebrune's residence, adopted the simplest possible tactic: he declared that 'he had not done anything nor had he seen any of the turmoil and emotions of Paris and even in the rue Saint-Honoré itself he had only seen a corpse'.[22] Occasionally the witnesses were a little more subtle in that they admitted to having been there but were not able to identify anyone present. That was the stand taken, for example, by the laundress Marie-Françoise Lecomte, who had also been at the market. In that centre of crowded gregariousness where no one can be a stranger for long, she saw everything and yet managed to declare that she 'didn't recognize anyone, there were only some ragamuffins, men, boys and all sorts of people she did not know'.[23] The main priority for the witnesses was obviously not to give anything away to the inquiry.

In spite of their basic caution the witnesses' accounts convey a true account of the actual conditions in which the events took place. One person can only remember a face ('He looked like an *Ecce Homo*'). Another recalls the colour of a torn suit. The facts are always reported haphazardly, without connection, and in the heat of the moment – almost as though it were impossible to shake off the immediacy of the events. The court clerks meticulously recorded all these fragmentary snatches of narrative: 'He went down to see what was happening and heard tell that this man had stolen a child.' 'He only followed the crowd and heard tell that the man was hiding in a laundress's house.' 'He had not known anything about the uprising but that all the market women were talking about it.' 'She had heard in the wash-house that the woman Eustache . . .'. The account is composed partly of traditional, word-of-mouth street gossip and partly of a mass of random detail, all thrown together with no attempt at classification or order. Everything was given equal value and it is clear that some of the statements were only included because of the obvious desire on the part of the police to reveal additional information that might only appear after double-checking all the statements later. Neither is there any discernible order within individual accounts. The story is built up from a succession of vignettes which were either true or presented as such. The account drawn from these statements remains fragmented and is never completely tied up into one coherent whole. Different levels keep appearing and occasionally a detail of gesture or colour, whose meaning is not immediately clear, leaps out as though suddenly magnified. These witnesses' accounts have the same characteristics of spontaneity and cunning as a street rumour or the echo of the city itself with its disjointed mixture of truth and hearsay.

There is one other important source of information coming, as it were, half-way between the press reports and the eye-witness accounts: this is to be found in the contemporary diaries and chronicles. The best and most prolific of the chroniclers were d'Argenson and Barbier, who recorded and commented on the events of the revolt as they were happening. The affair was not simply an item of news for them but prime material for their work. The dismissive indifference of the journalists was not for them; on the contrary, they fed off minute details. And in contrast to the eye-witnesses, the diarists never left their desks. Far from being blinkered by the immediacy and proximity of events, their clear and more or less avowed intention was to provide a coherent picture of those days of confusion and to draw a lesson from them. The chroniclers drew on a rich variety of sources whose distinctive traces reappear throughout their writings. They set their pace by the input of fresh information which constantly altered or completed the picture as much, if not more than the rhythm of the events themselves.[24] This influx of new information led to a rather breathless style, slightly reminiscent of the gossip sheets. 'News reaches me from Paris . . .'. 'There is a rumour that . . .'. 'We have just learnt . . .'. 'Yesterday some people told me . . .'. 'I have seen some letters . . .'.[25] The diarist relied on these latest items of information and changes in the situation and the constant amendments lend veracity to the story. The writer often adopts certain stylistic devices such as the use of the indefinite or stock phrases such as 'it is said that . . .' to imbue his chronicle with the fleeting authenticity of a news item.

Style alone does not provide solutions, and the diarists too were hard put to it to offer a coherent account of the revolt. The marquis d'Argenson lived through the events at a distance. Geographically he was some distance from Paris during the events of May, on his country estate where he managed to keep himself fully informed having the advantage of a brother who was the Minister for Police. D'Argenson was also at a distance politically. This great philosopher lord saw the violence in the capital as an illustration of the truth of his own opinions. Since retiring from public office after a brief spell at the Ministry for Foreign Affairs, the former minister had one overriding obsession: the denunciation of what he scathingly called 'the regime'. He could not find words harsh enough to use against Louis XV's 'spendthrift anarchy' or against 'the King and his reign of deception'. Suffice it to say that d'Argenson was all too ready to interpret the uprising as the beginnings of a far more radical upheaval. Some time later, when discussing the general discontent permeating the kingdom, he turned his thoughts towards the Glorious Revolution of 1688 and prophesied: 'All the elements are volatile. A disturbance can become a rebellion and a rebellion, total revolution . . . .'[26] Nevertheless he was rather too obsessed by the inexorable course of events, which he was convinced was imminent, to be able to explain what was happening before his eyes. When it came to it, this strongly opinionated man was capable of strange vacillation.

> 26 May: News comes from Paris that there have been frequent uprisings since my departure, especially on the 23rd of this month when there were as many as four on the same day, and they are all to do with some children having been arrested. It is quite incomprehensible.

By 27 May he seems to have formulated his own explanation of the affair. 'The people are still convinced that the constables are taking their children and there are riots in all four corners of Paris and simultaneously in the centre.' The marquis certainly had no great regard for the people, but who is to be believed?

> 28 May: No one seems to want to believe that the archers did not in fact arrest any children and that the whole thing is a figment of the shocked and outraged people's imagination. Astonished questions are being asked on all sides. Why would children be arrested in the first place? Why should they be taken rather than able-bodied men and women capable of populating the colonies? On the other hand how could people believe it if there is no truth at all in the story? Who would incite and provoke such frequent, widespread rioting?

Three days later he heard that the rioters had been manipulated 'by some people ranking above the populace', but he did not give the theory much credence; 'I cannot begin to explain the mystery.' On 18 June, he records as noteworthy 'that the people have not ceased fighting, looting and shouting for one moment. Disturbances in the past have always ceased for a few hours around lunch-time but not this time.'[27] It is clear that d'Argenson was determined to exercise his critical faculties freely in the matter, but in fact he did so to very little effect. The events of which he remains one of our best sources of information appear to have left him unusually indecisive. It is almost as though he were hampered by his own knowledge and became so involved in trying to unmask the powerful forces moving in the shadows behind the street demonstrations that he did not manage to formulate a constructive account of the revolt itself.

Barbier too displays a similar hesitancy and yet he is an altogether different kind of witness. For forty-five years this parliamentary lawyer specializing in legal consultancy kept a Paris chronicle. He was a great notable and had access everywhere, particularly to the Châtelet and the Council Chambers. Ironic and sceptical, he had a passion for news and turned his talents to accumulating an extraordinary sociological knowledge of the city.[28] He was equally nonplussed by the events, yet he had been the first to spot what was happening at the end of 1749: 'People have been abducted from the streets of Paris over the last month . . .', which is not to say he was convinced by the stories surrounding the arrests: 'It is one of the people's fairytales.' Barbier knew for several months that something was going on in Paris but he was never able to assess the affair properly or to distinguish between rumour and fact. In his journal, he frequently changed direction on the same page. One minute he was disinterestedly reporting events: 'They say that in Paris constables in disguise are roaming various districts . . .', then in virtually the next paragraph he was obviously accepting the story as fact: 'Today, Saturday morning of the 16th of the month a child was deliberately taken from the rue de Fourcy and port aux Veaux district . . . .'

Barbier's diary following the events' developments was written along the lines of an official inquiry. His search for the truth produced new and often contradictory details every day. The diarist was attempting to encapsulate the events for posterity but he never decided on one final version. As a critic he wanted to distinguish the truth from the merely plausible and the plausible from the unthinkable, but both the abductions and the revolt remained enigmatic to him. He found the abductions incomprehensible: 'There is no way of understanding it.' The revolt threw all his knowledge of the capital into question: 'The incident is particularly extraordinary since the people of Paris are usually mild and quite peaceful. Such troubles have not been seen for forty years, not even during the years of high bread prices.'

Of all the contemporary witnesses, Barbier provides by far the fullest, most coherent and detailed account. He lists the factors leading up to the events and probably knew as much as could be known about the whole affair. Yet, for all that, his account is founded on uncertainty, lacks organization and fails to draw any firm conclusions.[29]

Thus from one source and another the essentially untellable story of a street commotion is unfolded with nobody knowing quite what to say about it all. It is understandable that the events of 1750, though negligible when compared with other momentous events,[30] have so intrigued both contemporaries and the historians who came after them.

2

Orders in the City

On the whole there is a general consensus of opinion in society as to the importance of peace and public order and the themes are constantly aired in continuous, loquacious public discourse. Both values are constantly being invoked by the police, the government, the crowd and individuals alike and are generally proclaimed to be indispensable to the smooth functioning of any society purporting to be exemplary. This is, however, a delusion, since peace and order are liable to be threatened at any given moment.

For the fact that there is general agreement on the necessity for maintaining peace and order does not mean that individual representations of these concepts are equally unanimous. Although the common aspiration is a shared one, conflicting interests in the city give rise to a variety of perceptions of order and disorder which are sometimes complementary but more often in opposition to each other. It only needs an atmosphere of fear to prevail or an accidental rupture of the surface equanimity and these divisions become patently obvious. One incident can provoke rival and sometimes violently opposed reactions. Indeed two such incompatible versions of public order took shape and came into conflict during the days of May 1750. The authorities perceived the uprising as a menacing disruption by the very nature of its existence, whereas the people saw it as an attempt to re-establish order after the disruption caused by the police. These interpretations are opposite and yet both in a sense are true. The most perceptive commentators, in particular the lawyer Barbier, attempted to respect both points of view.

In reality the origins of the uprising date from long before 1750. Since the end of the seventeenth century the authorities responsible for public order had been concerned at the spectacular growth of the city's shifting population. In 1702, a figure of 9,000 beggars was mentioned; in 1750, 15,000. In an effort to halt this ominous tide, legal measures for cleaning up Paris were multiplied. The sheer number of these edicts and ordinances implies that they were ineffective, but the persistence of the authorities in issuing them shows that they were compelled to do something in the face of unacceptable reality. The method of dealing with this uncontrollable mass of people was simple. Drastic recommendations from the police, which have been kept handwritten, asserted the need for 'operations of selection and discrimination.

Selection and discrimination: the words suggest the urgency of the situation but therein also lay the problem. Once the vagrants had been picked out and isolated their fate had still to be decided. Expulsion would only rid the capital of them in the short term since they would soon reappear in Paris. The standard punitive sanctions of prison and the galleys seem to have offered a very limited solution, possibly because these options were unpopular in a society that felt responsible for its poor.[1] This feeling of guilt might also explain why the major repressive measures at the beginning of the eighteenth century (three important edicts in 1701, 1702, 1709 and one ordinance in 1706) should have made tentative moves towards introducing an element of social assistance into the politics of arrest. There was, for example, the attempted rehabilitation of vagrants by the establishment of public workshops, as happened after the terrible winter of 1709 when a large influx of beggars descended on a city already exhausted by famine and disease. However one should not overstress the element of social conscience since the statutory decrees consistently exhorted workers, merchants and servants not to offer protection to the poor.

There was one other solution to the problem and this sought to extract the greatest possible benefit for the kingdom from the situation. Why not use the floating population as recruits to populate and exploit the American colonies? The idea of compulsory emigration took shape during the Regency and was particularly prominent throughout the years of heavy colonial investment in Law's time as Controller General. In 1717, an edict drafted by the Naval Inspector de la Boullaye proposed the deportation of all able-bodied vagrants and beggars.[2] In the following year the Bicêtre prison, along with several others, drew up a list of undesirables for the attention of the police. Vagrants were not the only ones to appear on the list, which also featured contraband salt-merchants and others guilty of fraud, prostitutes and all kinds of young delinquents. In November 1718 an order was issued to the constabulary urging them to act with zeal so that 'the King may send all those fit to

be of use to the colonies'. Another declaration of 1719
lent further weight to the intention because it gave
judges the power to send all those under sentence of the
galleys to serve in the colonies instead. Many of those
who fell into this category were serving detention
orders and included former apprentices, craftsmen and a
large number of young people. The 'discrimination'
that was initially supposed to have been exercised was
thus soon forgotten. Under the weight of pressure
exerted both by the administration and the business
community, the deportation movement was on the
point of going out of control. In 1720 the scenario of
child abductions and subsequent uprising was briefly
enacted for the first time and thirty years later the
memory of it was still alive.

The capital was alarmed, not so much by the repressive measures in principle, but rather by the excessive
zeal with which they were carried out: 'They were
taking all sorts of people *indiscriminately*'. It was this lack
of discrimination between people's status, which existed
even at the lowest levels of poverty, that was causing
the greatest anxiety throughout Paris. Everywhere there
were stories of children being abducted or of forced
emigration to America. In April 1720 an uprising took
place 'against the archers who were taking all sorts of
people indiscriminately'. There was great resentment at
the casualness of the police who, enthused by the re-
wards offered by the Compagnie des Indes, often did
not even bother to observe the basic legal formalities
and were thus seen to be violating common human
rights. Parliament's secret council meeting at the time
acknowledged this popular resentment: 'The people
were very bitter against them and with good reason

since it is an infringement of liberty not to be able to set foot out of doors without being arrested and sent to Mississippi.'[3] The general alarm was sufficiently great for a new royal ordinance to address the problem over the following weeks and try to restore a semblance of order acceptable to both factions. After their arrests, vagrants were to be questioned by a police officer before their futures were decided. The archers on their part were to perform their duties in public only in brigades under the command of a constable and in uniform. This fragile balance did not restore confidence for long between the people and the police, nor did it succeed in establishing any commonly acceptable ground rules.

Thus a situation of latent crisis bursting intermittently into violence was established in Paris. The factors of the problem were to remain unchanged throughout the last century of the Ancien Régime. The town did not cease to attract wanderers and vagrants, who came from far and wide hoping for a refuge, some income or, failing that, the companionship of other outcasts. Needless to say, such hopes were dashed more often than not. The presence of this ever-increasing, pervading, anonymous multitude, which was grudgingly accepted under normal conditions, became intolerable when times were hard – particularly when dearth seized the capital in its grip in 1725, 1726 and again from 1738 to 1741. Even the rumour of a grain shortage as in 1747–48 was alone enough to sow the seeds of anxiety. Government and police appeared to be powerless in the face of this threat. They were out of their depth and vacillated between several possible, contradictory solutions, which they then put into effect simultaneously: assistance, compulsory labour, deportation and, above all, imprisonment.

Seemingly incapable of deciding on one policy, the authorities allowed these brutal, semi-legal measures to take their course and in the process probably succeeded more in antagonizing the people of Paris than in intimidating the beggars.

The edict of 12 November 1749 should be seen in the context of this overall background of annually mounting insecurity. It could at least claim the virtue of clarity in its brutal directness: 'His Majesty commands that all beggars and vagrants found in the streets of Paris, be they in churches or at church doors, in the countryside or surrounding districts of the capital, of whatever age or sex, shall be arrested and taken to prison, there to be detained for as long as shall be deemed necessary.' The tone of the document is harshly repressive and the call to order goes beyond the capital to encompass the whole country. The marquis d'Argenson was half approving, yet noted sardonically in his journal: 'The order has gone out to arrest all the beggars in the kingdom at once. The constabulary are to take action in the provinces just as in Paris, where they are sure the vagrants will not reappear since they will find themselves surrounded on all sides.'[4] Although the meaning of the edict was perfectly clear, the methods authorized to carry it out were far less so and left a great deal to individual interpretation and improvization.

The man in charge of executing this grand design was more noted for his zeal than for his scruples. The Lieutenant General of Police, Berryer, was one of the marquise de Pompadour's creatures and had been installed by her in 1747. He was a 'new' man, a man of power, 'insolent, hard, brutal'. He rapidly became hated, not only for his own sake but because he also reflected some of the constant, vociferous hostility directed at his patron, the all-powerful Royal Favourite. She 'had wanted the position to be occupied by a man who was entirely hers. This man was completely devoted to her, which made him odious to the general public from the start.'[5] Nicolas-René Berryer was altogether too concerned with displaying his energy and the efficiency of his administration in high places and seems consequently to have misjudged the scope and parameters of his task.

He wanted to achieve instant, tangible results and to that effect he had put a new team together within days. Without considering the possible consequences, he personally directed the inspectors and constables to act fast and decisively in the matter. His position made him virtually all-powerful; the police henchmen were entirely at his personal beck and call and worked only 'when the Lieutenant wishes to employ them'. Later, during the official inquiry, one of these same policemen was to declare: 'A man must work or die of hunger.' Berryer was well aware of the power invested in him and was also adept at playing on his men's greed. When it was suggested to him that the constables should be paid at a flat rate instead of by the number of arrests, his harsh reply was: 'That would be work fit for canons; I don't want sinecures; I only part with money when the goods are delivered.' During the official inquiry, Faillon, a cavalryman of the Watch, was to explain 'that he gave Monsieur Berryer a daily account of the previous day's captures and that if these had inadvertently included individuals with family and fixed abode, Monsieur Berryer, far from admonishing him, would approve of his actions as it was apparently perfectly in order to arrest children of artisans or bourgeois playing in the squares.'

The testimony of the men who actually carried out the orders unanimously affirmed the ruthlessness of the operation and these very men seem to have been the most sensitive to the possible consequences of such a policy. Indeed, most of them claimed to have expressed their reservations at the time, although it should be borne in mind that they were probably justifying themselves before the magistrates by laying all blame on the Lieutenant General of Police. Some of the men, while not ultimately refusing to obey orders, had nevertheless tried to secure their future positions in the matter. One Danguisy, for example, made his daughter keep a notebook in which she entered all the details of his arrests in case he ever had to give an account of them in court.[6]

However, the Lieutenant General also had to justify the trust placed in him by the Court and he would stop at nothing to achieve results. It is possible that he may have misread the situation and mistakenly but sincerely believed that public approbation was behind him. After all, for months he had been receiving complaints from parents whose delinquent children were beyond control, actually asking the police to exert their authority. During recent years the volume of petitions and detention orders had been steadily increasing.[7] Berryer may well have made an error of judgement in failing to recognize the enormous difference between the individual seeking the help of his sovereign's paternal power in solving domestic problems and the arbitrary imposition of unjustified indiscriminate violence by the police and their occasional collaborators on the streets of Paris. The uprising of 1750 was born out of his profound incomprehension.

Trouble Unleashed

From the moment of the very first signs of disturbance there arose two distinct and conflicting concepts of order, each having its own internal logic and, despite their opposition, both sharing a vision. Naturally each camp blamed the other. From the Parisians' point of view, children should not be abducted under any circumstances, not even in the name of the law. The police, on the other hand, upheld the view that not even the liberation of the children and the punishment of those responsible for their arrest justified revolt against the King's authority. These two opposing views arose, however, from a shared perception of disruption and the belief held by both parties that life in the city should be peaceful and harmonious. The actions and constant presence of the police in the capital throughout the eighteenth century were always motivated by their desire to maintain this harmony. His Majesty's loyal subjects shared the same concern for peace and tranquillity. Therefore any rupture of this common aspiration must perforce be due to malicious external influences. The city appeared to be under threat.

The police not only took action to quell and suppress agitation but reported at length on their actions, both verbally and, above all, in the form of copious files, reports, memoranda and notes scribbled in margins. These commentaries, ranging in style from lively to pedestrian, terse to loquacious, all serve to build up a picture of the events within which each incident has its own place and significance. It is through this varied police commentary that the obscure daily eruptions of violence begin to take shape and to be seen as part of a far more widespread plot justifying repressive counter-measures. The police were trying to shed light on incomprehensible elements and to that end they convinced themselves that their version of events was the correct one. Being working professionals rather than armchair experts, they also needed to furnish their theories with solid proofs since their job was to produce facts leading to convictions. The police interpretation of the 1750 uprising therefore comprises not only the events they witnessed but equally what they chose to believe to be the underlying truth that reduced the incomprehensible outburst of violence to the level of a reassuringly ordinary protest.

Their basic premise was that disorder cannot exist without someone being guilty of causing it. The police knew perfectly well what had enraged the people of Paris and for the most part they freely admitted it, some of them even going so far as to deplore their colleagues' actions. However this was rarely put forward as a valid explanation for the revolt. Since, in their view, collective aggression and street violence could never be justified in themselves, they drew on a powerful set of unshakeable beliefs to explain the causes of such a situation. One of the strongest of these theories was that if peace was under threat and violence unleashed, it had to be the work of malign forces infiltrating the social body in Paris. The forces of law and order had always been quick to recognize these pernicious invaders.

> One thing I am told which I can hardly believe is that at the height of the disturbances . . . there were three or four individuals pretending to be drunk who were handing money out to people saying, 'Here, my friends, here are six francs, go and buy some broom handles to attack these rascals with.' If that were true it means there

were secret leaders to the sedition. Only time and further information will reveal the truth of the matter.[8]

Despite his careful wording, prosecutor Gueulette, who recorded this rumour of 23 May, did not have much faith in the existence of 'men in black' supposedly emerging from the shadows to lead the uprising. Gueulette was an expert on Parisian law and order, an assiduous commentator on legal affairs and the author of a very full memoir of the events of spring 1750, which was furnished with many first-hand accounts. Clearly he was not convinced by the enigmatic presence of those archetypal *agents provocateurs* who were almost too perfect and certainly too elusive to be credible. However, neither did he believe that the people would erupt into violence without being led to it and he looked for the perpetrators in what, from the evidence, seemed to be the likeliest places.

Firstly among the vagabonds and prostitutes who had been the first victims of the 1749 edict and who consequently nursed a grudge against the police: 'There was some reason to believe that a certain number of rogues and villains, many of whom had been arrested and taken to Saint-Louis, had decided after their release to take revenge on the constables and archers by accusing them of abducting children to repopulate the colonial islands.' These 'bad apples' were only the tip of the iceberg of a criminal underworld, which thrived on civil disorder and actively encouraged it. Gueulette's hypothesis had the virtue of simplicity and was predictably confirmed by many grass-roots items of information. Inspector Roussel was working on the spot and kept his eyes and ears open although he already knew what he was looking for. On the evening of 23 May he was drawn to a potentially troublesome gathering of people in the rue des Petits Champs: 'They say it all started with one delinquent saying, "Look, there's one of those child abductors!" And a dozen people congregated.' Thus the criminal underworld was behind the uprising, certainly because they hoped to gain something from it. Roussel goes on to say, 'I posted various persons in different districts who all reported back that ordinary people's imaginations are growing daily . . . and I have no doubt that these rumours spreading into the countryside are attracting many thieves and rogues to Paris. The crooks and rabble-rousers have been stirring things up and encouraging people's gossip for four days now.'[9]

Crime attracted crime and bred on the very anxiety it sowed in the minds of a credulous people. If nothing was done it threatened to infect the whole of Paris. These theories were propounded again and again to the point of obsession and they make it clear why the police, blinkered by their own preconceptions, chose to see 'secret leaders' and 'experienced rabble-rousers' everywhere. Although in reality they fully understood the true complexity of the affair, they nevertheless became obsessed with the idea of a plot. The ideal of building the good of the people on the basis of strict administration of a morally healthy city was not abandoned, but it gave way temporarily before the more urgent problem at hand: the upsurge of evil in the urban society of Paris required instant repression.

All of a sudden the familiar image of society became clouded. In upholding their vision of public order, the police were no longer able to distinguish clearly between good and bad, evil or misguided motives. The uprising was treated like a sudden, unpredictable epidemic that had to be attacked simultaneously on all fronts. Clearly there were certain groups of people and particular occupations that were more suspect than others. These groups, being by tradition unruly, were more liable to infiltration by malefactors who could use them to disseminate rumour and violence throughout the city. After the disturbances, Inspector Poussot made enquiries in the rue de Cléry and rue de Bourbon: 'It would be too difficult to pinpoint the guiltiest parties amongst the master carpenters and journeymen in these streets since they are all guilty to some extent. These people have always been rebellious and it would be a good idea to make an example of some of them in the area.' He added a note in the margin: 'It will be hard to find anyone to give evidence against them since they are all in league with each other and it would be no use looking for informers.'[10] Poussot surely did not fabricate this idea of the solidarity within a particular job or district. No doubt he had come up against it before in the course of his work and was in a good position to recognize it again. But he was unable to interpret solidarity as anything other than evidence of complicity.

All existing social tensions became open to reinterpretation and began to be seen as elements in a wider scheme of subversion. A commonplace incident of conflict at work turned sour could become, without any further proof, a sign of participation in the uprising. On 23 May, two workmen, Pierre Tournier and Nicolas Passerat, who were vainly seeking a wage increase from their boss, insulted him and they came to blows. This was enough in itself for them to be arrested and brought before the instructing magistrate as though the incident could not possibly be an isolated one but must in some way be connected with the more widespread sedition.[11] The typically confused logic behind such a reaction indicates that, as far as the forces of law and order were concerned, the danger was no longer localized but virtually omnipresent throughout the city, and the people of Paris had to be protected against themselves.

In this atmosphere of widespread suspicion, the most entrenched prejudices re-emerged and came into their own. As we have already seen, the traditionally volatile areas and occupations were highlighted and became obvious and convenient targets for suspicion. The police imagination was haunted by shadowy, elusive groups of people. Their fear of seeing an influx of vagrants and delinquents into the city was exacerbated by their belief that behind this flow of people there were criminal organizations that were far more of a threat to society for being truly lawless and anarchic. These robber bands were both a myth and a reality still powerfully present in people's memories. The names of the 'famous robbers' went back in an unbroken line to the beginning of the eighteenth century. In 1750 it was still being noted in police documents that a certain individual was suspected of having belonged to Nivet's gang (1728–1729) or Rafiat's (1731–1733). The gangs never disappeared completely, either in fact or from public memory. The legend was certainly kept alive in pamphlets, ballads and folk-tales, and the fact that the police were still determined to track them down after a gap of twenty or thirty years shows that they still placed great importance on the phenomenon of these robber bands, which seemed to defy the passage of time.

Why did the gangs inspire such fear? The thieves

followed the fairs in summertime and in winter they converged on the capital where they cut purses with the regularity of seasonal workers. There was nothing very unusual in that. Perhaps the gangs caused such anxiety to the police because they appeared to have the goodwill of the ordinary populace behind them, sometimes actively so. At the end of the 1720s, Philippe Nivet, called Fanfaron, was able to escape from the archers several times with the help of local people before his final capture.[12] Certainly, by their very presence, the robbers emphasized the underlying antagonism between people and police. The main problem, however, was that the gangs spread a network which appeared to be virtually indestructible. No sooner was one arrested and made an example than another appeared to take his place. Inspector Roussel, being an old hand at matters concerning public order, was very aware of the existence of these shady companions who were constantly reinventing the great criminal organizations of the past. Women played a central role in their society. No robber was without his wife, mother, sister or mistress. Equally, every whore was attached to some thief. Women often provided the only contact between bandits who had been isolated by exile or prison and, in their own way, they ensured the survival of the group. Police investigations were frequently directed towards these women. No interrogation failed to identify a robber's female companion, whether the relationship lasted for a day or a lifetime. No police raid ignored the more renowned prostitutes and pickpocket girl-friends who formed the most stable elements of criminal society, whom the police tracked down in the hope of being led on to bigger prey. The fact that interrogations of women multiplied, albeit unfruitfully, in June and July 1750 is significant in that it demonstrates that the examining magistrate was also convinced of the presence of the invisible, underworld foe.

Police Misconduct

Throughout the whole of the judicial inquiry, which opened on the day after the revolt, the line of cross-examination followed the basic premise that the crowd was the guilty party of the May riots. But the witnesses' testimony frequently suggested an alternative version, namely that police misconduct was the cause of all the disturbances. Similar arguments were used in support of both these opposite theories.

Just as the investigators sought to pinpoint the sub-versive activities of criminal organizations, the people were pointing to the presence of 'bad apples' in the police force and in doing so they were probably not mistaken. There was, for example, one Antoine Severt, known as 'Parisien', who had worked for many years for the two police inspectors Durot and Poussot. The two officers worked in tandem and Parisien answered exclusively to them, being paid 600 livres a year for his services. It was common knowledge that he was a police henchman and spy, and he was so detested that, signi-ficantly, some people believed that it was he and not Labbé who had been murdered on 23 May. It is not entirely clear where Parisien's loyalties lay. When asked 'if he had not already spent time in the Conciergerie and Châtelet prisons' he replied that 'Yes, he had been involved in the Lalande case and that the said Lalande, who was a member of the Rafiat gang, had, at the instigation of a certain Poulot, charged him, Parisien, with a murder for which he was duly imprisoned. In fact he had never killed anybody and had not even known Lalande before going to prison, and eventually Lalande had been put to the wheel and confessed that Parisien was innocent and that it was Poulot who had put him up to making the false accusation for his own private revenge . . .'.[13] We can never know the whole truth behind this jumble of explanations but they do at least demonstrate that the accusation was plausible in the eyes of the magistrates as well as those of ordinary people. It is certainly the case that during the Ancien Régime, as in many other periods of history, the police made use of informers and collaborators whenever possible.

What of Poussot himself, the paymaster of Parisien, Labbé and many other informers? The crowd had searched in vain throughout Paris for him and his men hoping to deliver some rough justice, a dubious honour, which Poussot boasted of to Berryer. During the inquiry, witnesses referred several times to his 'gang'. The term is unambiguous and, by implication, labels Poussot's behaviour as lawless. One member of his team was his mistress Geneviève Dion, called 'La Maréchale'. She was a reformed thief who had been recruited by the police and put in charge of spying on illegal lampoon pedlars and of the surveillance of prostitutes. Dion had never drawn a clear line between the practice and prevention of crime and brought all the methods of her previous activity to her new one: violence, blackmail, spying and extortion. She had the power to incarcerate people or release them from prison at her personal whim. For example, she once offered to release a woman named Geneviève Pommier, who had been imprisoned for selling forbidden fly-sheets, if she would agree to become 'a slave to her pleasures'. La Maréchale was eventually to become a victim of her own inflated ambitions and vicious appetites. Meanwhile her infamous activities and those of her acolytes were common knowledge and affected the reputation of the whole police force. When Labbé was being hounded by the crowds on 23 May, it was in the building where Poussot and his mistress had lived the year before that he sought refuge hoping to find friends and protection there. Moreover it was the hated memory of 'La Maréchale's gang' that spurred the crowd to hunt Labbé down to his lair.[14]

Thus the police had their own unsavoury characters and dubious network spread throughout the city and they were not above using methods which were undoubtedly abuses of their power.

Why were children being abducted from the streets of Paris? As we have seen, there are several possible and frequently contradictory answers to the question. But in all the theories the police emerge as the perpetrators and can in some cases be shown to have benefited from the crime in a very direct manner. The constables were paid on a bounty system for their captures. Sébastien Le Blanc, who was charged on the day after the riots, informed the examining magistrates that he was paid for arrests on a per capita basis: 'Twelve francs out of which he had to meet all incidental expenses such as hiring vehicles and archers to whom he paid fifteen sols each . . . and that there were times when he was left person-

ally out of pocket.'[15] The going rate was low and seems
to have inspired some of the police henchmen to force
the pace and exceed their already harsh orders in pursuit
of bonuses. And the venality did not stop with the
arrests. There is abundant evidence from parents who,
having been alerted by the police, found their children
in prison and had sometimes to pay dearly for their
release. Marguerite Simon saw her son taken with two
playmates before her very eyes in the Place Royale and,
despite enjoying the protection of a parliamentary councillor, took a fortnight and fifty-five sols to secure his
release from prison, added to which she had to pay for
his food throughout his detention. Georges Bachevilliers, a master button-maker, also had to wait two
weeks before securing the release of his fifteen-year-old
son who had been sent on an errand. He paid 'thirty-six
sols to gain entry and four livres sixteen sols for his
release', in spite of which the youth spent his time in
prison 'sleeping on straw and caught scabies from which
he is still not cured'. Barthélemy Lucas was forced to
borrow money to secure his child's release after seven-
teen days in prison. All in all there was a strong assump-
tion, which was shared by the magistrates, that several
members of the police force were motivated by profit
into less than scrupulous execution of their duties.
Councillor Severt for one was apparently convinced
that the constables had a special arrangement with the
clerks at the Châtelet prison, although he could not
prove it.

Irregularities within the police force, though serious,
were in no way exceptional. They were probably a
necessary mechanism in the functioning of an admini-
strative body which was never adequate to its task

despite the prestigious reputation which it held throughout eighteenth-century Europe. If this unscrupulous behaviour suddenly assumed such prominence, it was not that it was a new phenomenon in itself but that in 1750 it came to be seen in a different light and as a menacing symbol of a new police order.[16]

Thus far we have been referring to the police force as one homogeneous unit whereas in fact it was composed of two separate entities whose balance was shifting at that time. One branch of the force was composed of commissioners who were magistrates in charge of the general administration of particular districts in Paris and came under the direct authority of Parliament. Law enforcement and crime suppression were only a small part of their work as they were well known to everyone in their districts and people turned to them spontaneously for help in settling the ordinary conflicts of daily life. The commissioners' authority was firmly rooted in their knowledge of the community.

In contrast to these locally based police was the relatively new body of men established at the beginning of the eighteenth century by the then Lieutenant General of Police d'Argenson, father of d'Argenson the minister and diarist. This branch of the force answered to a very different description, both in its function, which was primarily repressive, and in the type of men employed. This body of police inspectors had been created in 1708 and came under the direct authority of the Lieutenant General who recruited and remunerated them as he wished. These policemen were not in charge of particular districts but specialized, rather, in specific issues of public order. They were omnipresent in the city and infiltrated even the humblest levels of society. Their

‚activities were both secret and a subject of common knowledge. They and their spies were to be found in every tavern, stairway and market place. They operated through a whole network of collaborators, whom they selected and paid at will. This system enabled police intelligence to infiltrate far deeper into the town since their informers were often ordinary members of the community who blended into the background. The growth of the spy network, coinciding as it did with an increase in the number of police officers in the first half of the eighteenth century, became the ugly face of a utopian vision of omniscience. The police had dreamt of being able to know all the secrets contained in the city, which would thus become revealed to itself.

The general public resented the increased police presence and were anxious at the sight of the inspectors and their henchmen taking over more and more of the functions of the original police. At least before they had been able to identify, thwart and, if necessary, fight against the familiar institutions. The archers of the Hôpital Général, for example, had traditionally been charged with the arrest of beggars and had frequently been in confrontations with the populace because of it. Like the underworld, the new brand of policemen were suspected of all kinds of dishonesty and with good reason. The commissioners had been warning the Lieutenant General for months about the growing feeling against the new police.[17] It was a wasted effort. Nicolas Berryer, dubbed 'the infamous Monsieur Beurrier' [Mr Butterman], followed his natural inclinations towards even tighter control and more repressive measures and he harshly increased the pressure without considering the consequences. Hence the ordinance of

November 1749, which did not differ in essence from any previous legislation except that the execution of the law was entrusted this time to the hands of the hated new branch of the police. Berryer was determined to succeed. He recruited more men, gave them their orders and urged them to be effective. At that point the pressure became intolerable. The old, familiar consensus which had formed around the maintenance of order was shattered. The people were at loggerheads with a police force which they no longer considered *their* police.

Did people really believe that the arrest of vagrants, old or young, marked the first signs of general repression in the capital? It is hard to say for sure, but Berryer's excessive ambition makes it credible. If young vagrants and the children of artisans and merchants could be taken indiscriminately, then nothing was secure and anything became possible. The violence of the revolt was a response to the police's misbehaviour.

3

The Rules of Rebellion

After the uprising, Barbier was to comment:

> Some examples will have to be made; otherwise on the one hand there would be a risk of allowing more widespread sedition, and on the other hand it would be dangerous to allow all that disturbance to go completely unpunished as it would be an admission to the people that they have potentially enormous power. They certainly had the upper hand throughout the whole business and had to be very carefully handled.[1]

By 24 May the chronicler realized that something out of the ordinary had taken place. Something had been expressed in the violence and turbulence and he clearly recognized the fact, though he deplored it.

It is hard to identify the significance of an uprising or even to describe it adequately, since it is all too easy to become overwhelmed by the turmoil and clouded by the mass of superfluous detail. Thus Taine was to conjure magnificent but hate-filled memories of the revolutionary mob of 1789 from which Gustave Le Bon in his turn attempted scientific analysis of crowd behaviour. Taine was driven by fear to write a defence of civilization whereas Le Bon was prophesying the age of the

51

masses and furnished recipes which were eventually
used by twentieth-century politicians. Both writers,
however, believed that a mass movement is only effective when all individual conscience and concept of order
is abandoned to the process of general unification.
People involved in uprisings have no goal other than
that of being together. They abandon themselves to the
dizzy irrationality which predisposes them to submit to
any charismatic ringleader. A crowd comes into being
simply for its own sake, with no plans or expectations
beyond the fact of its own existence.[2] Other historians
propose a diametrically opposite theory and look to the
will of individuals involved in the collective adventure
of rebellion. These historians are usually more interested in the social composition of the crowd than in
its behaviour. Their theory is that its meaning and
function can only be made clear by an understanding of
its social composition.[3] By following lines indicated in
some recent publications[4], we will attempt in this work
to distance ourselves from the two aforementioned
theories, both from that which regards crowd behaviour as having no significance beyond its own existence and from the idea that the dynamics of the events
themselves can be ignored in favour of a social analysis
of the crowd. We understand the revolt itself as a
persistent, a piecemeal, search for a meaning which is
not given at the beginning, and which only gradually
reveals its true significance.

It is necessary first to determine exactly who took
part in the riots. The rioters are usually referred to as
though they were one collective body with words such
as 'the people', 'the crowd' and, frequently, 'the rabble'.
These terms, while being universally accepted and even

employed by the rioters themselves during the inquiry, do not serve to describe or identify any particular groups of people. It is not easy to clarify the social composition of the uprising, not for any lack of witnesses – on the contrary, there is a relatively large amount of testimony but most of it is biased and says more about the beliefs of the authors than anything else. Inspector Roussel provided a good example of this intuitive sociology in his account of the evening of 23 May when he came across a group of people gathered in the rue des Petits Champs:

> I asked them what the problem was, and some told me that some constables had tried to arrest a child, while others said the child abductors had gone into hiding at the baker's. We went on our way ... but in a few minutes the group had become much larger and was attracting many servants in particular who passed by without speaking to us.

Should Roussel's opinion be taken as fact? He certainly knew the Parisian scene well, but his very knowledge led him too easily into unquestioning attitudes. He had the same impulse that drove his colleague Poussot to look for culprits in certain specific districts and trades.

Roussel also provided some rather more reliable material in the form of written reports on the intelligence that he directed his informers to gather in Paris during the two days following the uprising. On the face of it this report is a meticulous piece of work. Beside each name he wrote down his informer's observations and a list of the witnesses each had heard. But despite appearances, this document is also biased. Roussel had sent his spies out to collect information in the taverns

and at toll-gates and other such places where any con-
versations reported would almost inevitably reinforce
the police in their belief that the criminal underworld
had had an important part to play in the revolt. Roussel
even introduced for good measure a group of witnesses
to strengthen his own interpretation of events. These
were merchants, bourgeois and 'honest artisans' who
deplored the turmoil in the streets and the inadequate
number of law-enforcement officers. The report then
turns its attention to the social structure of the mutinous
crowd and springs no surprises in the roles ascribed.[5]

The list of suspects submitted to Parliament's General
Procurator and that of the accused brought before the
Court clearly confirms the contemporary analysis of the
revolt. Despite the fact that very few names appear on
both lists, the obvious implication is that the uprising
was the work of that shifting, unstable element of the
Parisian population that had long been considered a
permanent threat to security.[6] No real criminals were
discovered but at best a few disreputable fellows, one of
whom was to pay for his reputation with his life. Most
of those presumed guilty were street people comprising
a few beggars, some wandering pedlars, itinerant workers, a hawker, a bootblack, a chair carrier, a water
carrier, two soldiers of the Militia – in other words, a
sample of those casual jobs by which so many Parisians
survived on the edge of dire poverty. By contrast the
lists included no craftsmen nor any women despite the
mass of evidence that both these groups played a large
part in the events, the women in particular. In fact the
choice of suspects already presupposed a certain interpretation of the revolt.

Certainly most of those suspected or accused had

indeed been present at the scenes of violence, and the inquiry frequently confirmed that they were in fact guilty of the seditious talk and brutality of which they were accused. But they all knew that they had not been the only ones involved, simply the only ones to have been landed in the net. The good shopkeepers, bourgeois neighbours and honest workmen who had often been the ones to denounce the accused, had also had children abducted by the police. In fact these solid citizens had been those whose anger had first fuelled the hue and cry and angry gatherings which ignited each stage of the riots and they had been present at the most volatile and violent scenes.[7] But not one of their names appeared in the official inquiry – except one, Louis Devaux, a master locksmith, who as we will see, had played an important role during Labbé's capture. Clearly these people were protected by their status. They were respectable members of society, and the police made a clear distinction between them and the more humble populace. They were also more articulate than beggars and better able to evade their responsibilities. But there is more to it than that. The fact is that once the drama was over and tension evaporated the worthy citizens were anxious to put it all behind them and align themselves with the police version of the affair; partly because it obviously suited their interests to do so, but also probably because they found it hard to identify with the revolt once the heat of anger and emotion had passed. They knew very well that it was not only the 'populace' who had taken part in the looting, pillage and destruction, but after the event they could not imagine how they had become involved in that any more than in the siege of the commissioners' residences. At the time, there had probably been a unanimous desire to punish the constable Labbé 'as an example', as someone put it; but in retrospect the whole business – including the cruel murder in the street, the rough denuding of the corpse for souvenirs, the derisory mock execution before the murdered man's house, the threats against the police, against Berryer, against the King – was all complete anathema to them. The bourgeoisie were aware that during the height of the revolt they had rubbed shoulders with a profoundly alien culture, which, in the cold light of day, they found deeply threatening.[8]

We will never know the full details of those who joined the riotous crowd which was clearly an amalgam of very disparate elements. Even if we did know more, the knowledge would be of little use since there was no guarantee that people conformed to type under those conditions, in fact the opposite was usually the case. The surveyor Langlois, for instance, who took part in the turmoil in the rue St. Honoré on 23 May in the company of an usher and a musician, was undoubtedly a *petit bourgeois* and proud of it. Nevertheless he was heard to utter incredible threats. He told his two companions 'that if they would accompany him, they would go and kill a constable at his house'. And later, in front of two of Berryer's clerks, Langlois, 'scenting blood', went further saying 'that they must treat those rascals like that villain being murdered. When the two asked him why, he answered "because your master is a scoundrel".' Did Langlois remember all his bluster after the events? In any case the magistrates chose not to pursue his arrest even though he had been denounced.[9] Langlois had been behaving out of character, or rather his uncharacteristic behaviour did not fit the preconceived picture formed by the police and the judiciary, which allowed them to treat the affair as a run of the mill protest.

We cannot conclude nevertheless, as Taine or Le Bon might have done, that emotion and violence are enough in themselves to fuse individual attitudes and assumptions into a common, collective insanity. If the uprising drew so many people from so many levels of society, it was not because of the work of professional agitators either. Rather it was because beyond the repetitious movements, cries and gestures, the revolt did offer the individuals it attracted something shared. There was a common goal, certainly, but more than that, a language which developed at the very heart of the uprising and which provided each individual with his or her own rationale. The events unrolled like a play that takes its framework from tradition but is improvised and scripted by the actors. The development was not a random affair however; the rioters themselves chose their locations and forms of expression and in exercising this choice they were constantly in the process of creating the significance of their own protest.

Processions in Town

At first sight the turmoil seemed to be everywhere. The riot appeared to be shapeless, made up of a series of episodes, isolated in time and space, which erupted in a disconnected way rather than as a linked chain of events. Each of these sporadic outbursts arose from unpredictable and uncontrollable, isolated incidents. Although some of the suspects were accused of reappearing at various rebellious scenes throughout Paris, the *whole* city was never involved at any one time. Each separate episode has its own anecdotal history, but there is another story to tell when they are taken as a whole. The common enemy, apart from the child abductors, was consistently and clearly identified as being the police who were so heavily involved in the affair. There were countless accusations and threats against the constables, the archers, the inspectors and their spies, and sometimes the simple presence of a squadron of police passing by was sufficient for crowds to gather and violence to be unleashed.

However, the violence was not completely formless and haphazard. The incidents themselves occurred at random, but in each case there seems to have been a common pattern of events culminating in a procession of rioters ending up in front of one of the police commissioners' residences. On 16 May a crowd chased and stoned the Swiss Guard from the faubourg Saint-Antoine to Commissioner Rousselot's residence. The crowd had picked on two fellows in the Saint-Lazare district and eventually brought them to Commissioner Regnard's residence. The constables who had been surprised with their cart by the crowd in the rue des Nonnains-d'Hyères sought refuge with Commissioner Rochebrune in the rue Geoffroy-l'Asnier. On 22 and 23 May, two suspects whom the Watch had taken great pains to protect were hunted and captured near the faubourg Saint-Denis and ended up at Commissioner Defacq's residence in the rue Saint-Martin escorted by a crowd of 'over four thousand jeering people'. (The figure was probably exaggerated.) Nicolas Niveltel, the soldier who had provoked the aggressive rage of onlookers near the Pont-Neuf, eventually found himself under siege in Commissioner Delafosse's residence in the rue de la Calandre. Finally, in the last violent scene of the uprising, the rioters took Labbé to Commissioner de la Vergée near the church of Saint-Roch.

There was no coincidence in this pattern. For fugitives on the run the commissioner's residence represented a safe haven where they could seek the protection of public authority; for the crowd at their heels, forcing a suspect into the magistrate's presence meant providing the bait for their redress. Both hunter and hunted believed that the commissioner would serve their best interests. At that time, the commissioner's residence played an important role in Parisian life. The house was known to everyone and was blatantly obvious with its walls covered in posters and public notices. It was there that the proclamations of arrests were placed, official celebrations announced and even notices placed of lost property. Sometimes an anonymous denunciation would be placed there by some malevolent hand. The house was accessible to everyone and acted as an information centre where news was exchanged and discussed. The commissioner himself fulfilled much the same function. Any incident, large or small, be it a question of unpaid rent, a stolen buckle, a scuffle or a violent crime, was brought to him in the first instance. He was nearly always available since the residence was also his family home. He heard complaints, calmed tempers, arbitrated and reprimanded when necessary, and occasionally took legal action or decided to make an arrest. He was a mediator, in constant contact with the local community, and he was required to be both authoritarian and protective at the same time. His particular role had evolved over years of custom and he was a reassuring, familiar figure.

The commissioner represented values totally opposite to those of the other members of the police force whom the rioters associated with the children's abductions, namely the inspectors, their henchmen and, above all, those informers who melted so effectively into the background of street life that one could never be sure of identifying them. By converging on the commissioner's residence, the crowd were hoping to clarify a situation which had become fraught with ambiguities. They were used to being listened to by the magistrate and hoped that he would restore the status quo for them. By their very choice of objective the rioters were therefore making a statement about what they wanted: a return to a normal, equable state of affairs. Often they did achieve the desired result. Commissioner Defacq, for instance, was able to provide reassurance. While asking the crowd to 'cease their chase', he also promised them that if one of the suspects brought before him 'was proved to have been guilty of abducting a child he would have him arrested. In this way he managed to quell the mob and then he called for a carriage to take the wounded'.[10] Initially Commissioner de la Vergée acted in the same way. There were times, however, when a commissioner shied away from the mediating role expected of him by the crowd and, frightened by the violence around him, chose instead to barricade himself against the crowd, and the opportunity for reconciliation was missed. Then the dividing line between good and bad police immediately became blurred, and the crowd turned their anger against this fallen symbol of authority who had refused to accept his designated role.

There was, therefore, a certain regularity in the behaviour of the crowd. But it is possible to look beyond modes of behaviour and, by examining the incidents closely, to discern patterns of action and organization which suggest that there was some logical order at work at the very heart of the chaos, enabling the rebellion to control the very violence it disseminated. We will attempt to demonstrate this by looking in detail at the most well-known and best documented episode of the uprising: this took place on 23 May. A close examination of that day's events may lead to a greater understanding of the whole affair.

Patterns of Violence

At about 9.30 that morning the riotous mob crossed the Quinze-Vingts market where people had been trading since dawn. The hunted Labbé and the pursuers at his heels did no more than run across the market square before disappearing into a nearby building. The whole scene lasted only a few seconds, and those who were there at the time asserted later, when questioned, that they could not remember any details. Nobody seemed to know anything about it, nor did they recognize anyone involved. This might be plausible were it not for the fact that all the witnesses referred insistently to the minutiae and demands of their jobs from which, if they were to be believed, nothing could have distracted their attention. In that intensely gregarious place, where everyone knew each other and the same families had been trading for generations, the crowd of rioters appar-

ently passed through like an alien phenomenon completely unrelated to life in the market. Seemingly the
most they could say about the revolt was that they were
aware that it had occurred. This was the line adopted by
Thomas Lamotte, an old street sweeper in the area who
remembered 'all those women running around and
barrels overturned'. His technique was a common one
under questioning. The trick was to avoid giving anything away to the investigators, who were clearly looking beyond mere information and were on the trail of
denunciations. This evasion was entirely reasonable in
view of the fact that everyone might ultimately have to
account for his or her own role in the affair. Far better
then to claim to have been too busy with other matters.
If they admitted to any knowledge at all of the affair, it
was never what they had seen with their own eyes but
always what they had heard tell after the event.

The witnesses were certainly not telling the truth.
While it is most unlikely that anyone followed events
from beginning to end, and while everyone was obviously taken by surprise, yet a profound knowledge of
their community would have allowed people to catch
instinctively at least the main outlines of the story. The
riot first appeared as a rumour. The people in the
market place knew there was something in the wind
before they saw anything specific. Moreover, they
knew exactly what it was that was afoot and were able
to spot violence in the air long before it erupted in their
midst. The butcher boys first gave cry to the trades-
women: 'Take cover, my friends, there's a ruction on
the way!' Roland, the water carrier, cried out, 'as
though to give warning: "Here comes the revolt!"'
Apart from the warning cries and the general bustle of

self-defence, there was also a feeling of heralding a familiar phenomenon. A riot was accepted as a recognized part of the social scene. This sense of familiarity reappears from one uprising to the next right up until the days of July 1789. People knew instinctively how to react to the announcement. There was no blind panic; people simply reacted promptly showing that they fully understood what was happening and the risks involved. Some chose to run away, like the herb seller who insistently told the judges how frightened she had been in an attempt to sound convincingly innocent. For others the first instinct was to secure their goods. The fishmonger Adrienne Boucher knew very well what a riot could lead to. At the first hint of trouble her reflex was to bury at the bottom of her wicker baskets the large knives she used for filleting fish.

Despite their protestations, people in the market place knew more about the pack who were chasing Labbé through the streets than they admitted, and must have been able to identify local people among them. They were all on their home territory, and although they feigned complete ignorance when the police were involved, they all knew each other by name or nickname, by sight or at least by reputation. The truth of this became apparent whenever police pressure was lifted. They certainly knew who the hunted man was and why he was being chased. The woman Olivier, who had tried to protect Labbé and had inopportunely directed him towards the Quinze-Vingts market, heard the cry, 'It's one of Monsieur Poussot's spies . . . whereupon the rabble fell upon both him and she who was leading him.'[11] The denunciation was more than a general expression of hostility towards the police, who had never been welcome in the closed confines of the market place. They were firmly naming the enemy since for several days there had been a growing conviction that Poussot and his spies were involved in the child abductions and they were being hunted down throughout Paris. Nobody admitted to having seen anything, yet most people agreed to having briefly noticed the colour of uniform which instantly identified the fugitive. The whisper ran from stall to stall in the market square where it was magnified like an echo chamber. Then, abruptly, the scene shifted from the square to the building where Labbé had hidden.

The building itself was like a city in microcosm.[12] It had five storeys comprising seventy households, eight shops, two butcher's stalls and several rooms, some of which were let to shopkeepers and others to working people such as tradesmen, servants and craftsmen. On the top floor there were the laundresses and an enormous attic which served as a dormitory for several workmen. It was a place where people both lived and worked, and many trades were to be found there. On the second floor, one woman sold roast meats while her neighbour sat behind an open door making children's garments. The ground floor was shared by a carpenter, a tripe seller and some butcher boys and was also used by a fishmonger to store the cod which she sold in the market. It was so dark and damp that they even grew chicory down there. The permeating odour in the building was a mixture of used crockery, wood-smoke, raw meat, cooking and household rubbish. There was constant noise coming from the corridors and attics, and rumour, gossip and snatches of conversation echoed around the building. The enforced propinquity and overspill of lives lived in such cramped conditions meant that nothing was secret for very long. Everybody knew everything about everyone. Every word spoken was swept up in the current of gossip flowing uninterruptedly along the stairways. The building was as overcrowded as the street and left no room for privacy. Every item of information was passed along the passages and corridors and through the doors and hatches. The lifestyle of the inhabitants rather than the design of the building prescribed its topography. The whole building was a cosy labyrinth whose ways had to be learnt.

Labbé knew its ways well. He had chosen that particular building overlooking the market because he hoped to find refuge there but he had not foreseen how brief a respite it was to be. Two years earlier, Labbé's paymaster, Inspector Poussot, had lived in the building with his mistress, La Maréchale. The woman Geneviève Olivier who helped Labbé to escape had been a close friend of theirs. In fact the two women had even shared their kitchen, which is not surprising when we learn that Olivier was 'what is known as a woman of the world who debauched young people'. Presumably the two women's shared predilection for vice was enhanced by their secret police work. The whole district and the inhabitants of the building in particular held bitter memories of their occupancy. In his choice of a bolt-hole and escort, Labbé had only managed to confirm the crowd's suspicion of him. At that point they were determined to catch him, not only because he was suspected of abducting the children but also because he had become a scapegoat on whom to settle old scores against a brutal and corrupt police force.

The fugitive soon realized his mistake: 'A terrified man in red with wild hair appeared on the stairs and begged us to save his life.' Labbé's companion, who had lost sight of him, immediately drew attention to herself in an inept attempt to allay suspicion by shouting 'Where is he? Where is he? He's not one of them. We're not part of them, that's a boy I delivered to the captain of the guard.' She herself tried to hide among the laundresses. She took off her bonnet and pretended to be ironing along with the others, but her ruse did not succeed for long. Labbé meanwhile had not found the strength to reach a friend of Geneviève Olivier's in one of the attics and had hidden under a bed in Dame Rozeau's rooms on the fourth floor. His pursuers had already flooded into the building and were blocking the exits. They were on their own territory and took instant possession, opening doors and rooting in corners at will without anyone seriously trying to prevent them from doing so.

Up to that point the action had been dictated by the life and layout of the building itself and the violence was following the pattern set by the hurly-burly of daily life in that community. Everything changed abruptly however when all at once a man appeared and announced: 'I am the master of this house.' Louis Devaux was forty-four years old, a master locksmith, and he had lived there for eighteen years. He was no ordinary tenant but the 'chief tenant' of the building and Quinze-Vingts market whose job it was to collect the weekly rents for the owner; he was a trustworthy man, used to handling large sums. (He spoke of 5,500 livres a year.) But his responsibilities did not stop at rent collection. Part manager, part Justice of the Peace, his job was to maintain order and, if possible, harmony in the place he was in charge of. Louis Devaux assessed the situation immediately and proceeded to impose his authority on all factions – not by force, which would have carried no weight with a crowd of rioters, nor later with the police, but by intelligence and a rapid grasp of the situation in hand. There were three major witnesses who later provided the bulk of what evidence we possess for this episode, and although they each had different versions of the affair, they all agreed on Devaux's skill in handling the matter.[13]

Louis Devaux basically sided with the crowd but he chose to control the violence and direct it away from the building. He used the power of his traditional role to the full, his first concern being to bring calm to the crowd by replacing the diffused rage around him with his own brand of authority. He told one man who was breaking a door down with a club: 'Steady, my friend, that's not the way. There's too much noise.' He took the lead announcing: 'I want these doors opened.' He managed to control the tumult while convincing the rioters that he was on their side. 'Because he was the chief tenant of this house . . . the crowd trusted him and let him go forward alone.' (In actual fact, they followed behind him at a distance.) After having searched in vain for Labbé in the attics, Devaux eventually discovered him in his hiding place and handed him over to three men with a detachment worthy of Pontius Pilate: 'There he is. Do what you want with him.' Did he have any real choice in the matter? Later, during the inquiry, when he was reprimanded for not having called the guard, he replied that had he done so he would certainly have been attacked and subsequent events bore him out in this.

But there was undoubtedly another reason why he did not do so. Devaux was not trying to represent the police force but simply to impose his personal authority.

He achieved his aim which was to bring some order to the situation but he did not attempt to go further and advocate appeasement. His only concern was to prevent acts of violence being committed on territory coming under his responsibility and he forbade the crowd to settle their account with Labbé there and then. Some people were holding the constable, 'whose face was covered in blood', and they were all for throwing him out of the window on the spot. Devaux intervened and gave some orders which precisely summed up his attitude: 'Don't throw the rascal out, take him away so that no business happens here.' He was treading a very narrow line, having at the same time to impose his authority, act in such a way as to antagonize neither rioters nor police and, above all, get rid of the problem. He managed it faultlessly, and the crowd followed his orders while he sent the tenants about their daily business and refused to allow his own craftsmen out of the workshop, ordering them to get on with their jobs.

Devaux's role did not come to an end with Labbé's departure. He still had a part to play but this time with an abrupt change of tune. Now that he had restored calm, the master of the building was able to settle his own scores. The arrival of the constable with his companion had been a public reminder that two years before the police had seen fit to encroach on his territory and install their dubious agents, unsavoury business and intolerable spies within the confines of his walls. By seeking refuge in the building, Labbé might have led people to believe that it was still collaborators' territory,

and now Devaux had to dispel all doubts on that score
and make good any harm done. So, after having
brought calm to the situation, Devaux stage-managed a
limited localized violence of his own, which he manipulated and controlled while ensuring that it was very
public. He found the woman Olivier on the top floor
where she had prudently taken refuge with her friend La
Denis, and there he vented his anger on her in ringing
tones: 'He did not want people collecting all kinds of
riff-raff in his house.' His words were deliberately
ambiguous but the meaning was clear – he would not
tolerate spies or any encroachment on his rights as chief
tenant. Straight away he set about organizing her expulsion from the building. He took care not to manhandle
Geneviève Olivier himself but pointed his finger at her
declaring loudly 'that she was a strumpet and no better
than La Maréchale herself'. Devaux knew exactly how
to make use of custom. Who better than the women in
the building to see Olivier off the premises under a
volley of abuse and draw crowds of passers-by to witness her public humiliation? He dispatched some of the
laundresses to alert people in the street. Marie-Françoise
Lecompte was one of them, and later on when questioned she told how 'Master Devaux had got her and
Dame Rambure and maybe fat Nanette too, to shout at
that Olivier woman out of the window and that she, the
witness, had put her head out of the window and called
out to Madame Devaux: "Look, there's Madame Olivier. Monsieur Devaux said she's that madam who used
to live here." And that the said Devaux then nudged her
with his foot and said, "Don't mention names, you silly
hussy."' Devaux was angry with the foolish girl who
had nearly given his plan away. The whole scene had to

appear to have been completely spontaneous for fear of reprisals.

Out on the pavement Olivier was surrounded by a little group of men and women who slapped her about and knocked her bonnet off. At one point it looked as though matters would go much further when the cry went up: 'She's a thief and one of La Maréchale's gang! She must die!' Eventually two butcher boys stepped in and let her make her escape, by which time it no longer mattered. Devaux had made his point and re-established order in his own domain by his own methods.

After that Louis Devaux disappears from the story. The focal part he played was due to particular circumstances of time and place. For a few crucial hours his institutional role, known and recognized by everyone, had given him the power to channel and orchestrate the revolt which formed itself fleetingly around him. But he was neither an agitator nor an intriguer as the judges, disorientated by the confusion of events, were inclined to believe was the case. Devaux's role was important because, far from choosing to take a lead, he found himself caught up in the maelstrom of the uprising. For a brief time his understanding of events provided a scenario which was acceptable to the insurgents and in which they could freely express their resentment in a form dictated by him. Then the crowd went on their way having no further use for him, and he in his turn had no further dealings with them.

Negotiations

The second climax of 23 May took place around Commissioner de la Vergée's residence in the rue St Honoré.

This was the scene of the riot's greatest violence when a running battle developed between the crowd and the officers of the Watch, ending in Labbé's murder before the church of Saint-Roch. The witnesses questioned during the judicial inquiry and the city's chroniclers all agree that this was the most violent and crucial episode of the rebellion. Both participants and observers saw the scene as being the culmination of a long period of increasing tension and also as a kind of denouement, a dramatic last act. Examined in detail, the evidence loses this homogeneity and is understandably more contradictory since a close reading of the testimony robs it of its total dramatic effect. The very wealth of fragmentary details reinforces the impression of confusion, violence and frenzy of the events themselves. The commissioner's own rambling testimony bears witness to the confusion. Louis Paillard, the commissioner's clerk who witnessed events from start to finish, gave an account which was thoroughly obscured by a mass of detail and even more muddled than that of la Vergée himself.

> The witness had been below at the door of the study which is next to the main gates when, having narrowly missed being hit by a stone and realizing the danger he was in, he withdrew upstairs to some conveniences which had a small window overlooking the courtyard from which he could see what was going on, and from there he saw that the Watch had fixed bayonets and had split into two groups, one on each side of the carriage gates, and the sergeant armed with a halberd was guarding the tavern, and the witness saw a little boy about ten years old, whom he did not recognize, slip into the courtyard through the broken glass door of the tavern when the sergeant pretended to point his halberd at him. The sergeant's name was Dunoix and he was a corporal at the toll-gate during the day and a sergeant on night

duties. At that moment the witness heard a shot from somewhere then another shot from under the carriage gates, which must have come from the crowds since the officers of the Watch were in the courtyard. So Duriez decided to order one of his soldiers to open fire and that shot drew another shot from the crowd which drew another from the Watch and then, seeing that the crowd was trying to force entry into the courtyard, Duriez, to stop them, ordered one or two more shots from his soldiers at which the crowd drew back into the street and continued throwing stones over the Commissioner's gate and that of the tavern for at least a quarter of an hour . . .[14]

Amongst all the confusion it is still not too far-fetched to discern again the threads of some kind of order. The behaviour of the rioters seems to have adhered to certain rules reflecting the values which they were apparently seeking to re-establish. In other words, they were somehow attempting to restore that common, unwritten code of conduct between Parisians and the police that had been transgressed. It is possible to see, beyond the chaos of words and gestures, a certain logical sequence of events in the rue St Honoré by which the crowd were trying to negotiate with the police.

After having captured Labbé, the rioters took him straight to the Police Commissioner's residence which was, as we have seen, a symbol of reassuring authority in Paris. The fact that the crowd chose this particular course of action indicates that they were seeking a re-establishment of order. The constable had been under suspicion for some time; he had been caught in the act of abducting a child, and therefore, in the normal course of events, he should be arrested and taken to prison pend-

ing a proper court hearing. The violence of the crowd
was not initially intended to threaten rebellion but was a
means of setting the normal procedure in motion and
restoring the customary balance between people and
police. This is certainly how Vergée and his adjutant
interpreted events when they undertook to escort Labbé
to the Châtelet: 'We answered in these terms and spoke
loudly so as to be heard by everyone, "My friends, I
will give you justice and commit this individual to
prison." They appeared satisfied with this answer.'[15]

For trust to be fully restored between people and
police, the wrong had to be publicly righted. Both the
commissioner and his clerk insisted on the fact that the
business had been conducted 'with open doors', in full
sight and earshot of the rioters, 'so as not to aggravate
the crowd'. This openness was in sharp contrast to the
secrecy which had shrouded the affair of the child
abductions from the beginning. The police were not
normally as open or public in their undertakings, but in
the particular atmosphere prevailing in the spring of
1750 openness was a necessary prerequisite for a return
to law and order. Foreseeing the likelihood of violence
on 23 May, Lieutenant General Berryer himself had
developed the theme in the rather cynical measures he
had recommended that very morning in a letter to
another commissioner, Regnard le Jeune:

> To dispel the anxieties which, however ill-founded they
> may be, appear to be growing among the populace, and
> to induce calm, it will be necessary for you, sir, to take
> these measures: if anyone is brought before you by the
> Watch or by the people accused or suspected of having
> tried to abduct a child, you must not detain him for a
> moment but send him instantly to the Conciergerie

whether he is guilty or not and make sure this is done in full view of the public and do not attempt to prevent them from following him there if they have a mind to.[16]

It was also necessary for roles to be clearly defined before calm could be fully restored. For, apart from holding Labbé and his colleagues responsible for kidnapping children, the greatest resentment was felt against them for the ambiguity of their position in the community. Labbé's allegiance to the police was only advertised in one particular, the red scarf recognized by so many witnesses with which he tried to cover his head for protection during his final flight. His skill had been his ability to merge into the Parisian background for greater freedom of movement. Even when he had come as far as the commissioner's office, Labbé was trying to conceal his identity by protesting that he was only 'a simple wine merchant's lad' and he waved a corkscrew in support of this story. Labbé was just one example of the general complaint against the police. Barbier was noting in his journal at the time that the secrecy surrounding police employees was causing great anger among people: 'All those people, whether they had been unable to escape and were attacked or mutilated or whether they had found refuge in private houses or more often with the commissioners, turn out to have been archers, informers or spies. What exactly were they doing?'[17]

At the point when Labbé was brought before the commissioner, it would still have been possible to restore order. La Vergée's public undertaking was all that was necessary to conclude the affair, but the delicate balance was promptly upset by a series of maladroit blunders. The Watch, who had arrived to escort the constable to prison, made two serious errors. Firstly, they wanted to clear the house of the rioters who had delivered Labbé although the commissioner and his clerk both 'opposed the move, not wanting to aggravate the crowd who were now pacified'.[18] Good sense did not prevail for long however, and the Watch forced the crowds back into the street, closed the carriage gates and arrested one of the rioters. This arrest was probably less damaging than the decision to remove the suspect and all subsequent dealings with him from the sight of the crowd, who wanted to keep an eye on matters. Predictably, the rioters then became enraged and attacked the commissioner's residence forthwith. The second mistake was made during the ensuing fracas by the sergeant, who was unwise enough to raise his halberd against the young lad who had managed to squeeze into the courtyard. The gesture was inept, to say the least, under the particular circumstances of the revolt, and was immediately followed by the first shot from the crowd and answered by one from the Watch. The affair was further mismanaged at that point when those who were in a position to act as intermediaries between the two camps promptly vanished from the scene. La Vergée barricaded himself into his private apartments the minute the crowd began attacking his house. He whose function it was to take part in all negotiations with the people thus abnegated responsibility and, in doing so, became suspect himself. His residence ceased to be neutral ground and became instead a target for collective vengeance. In fact that evening, after they had recaptured and murdered Labbé, the rioters considered returning to inflict some more definitive punishment on the commissioner for his treachery.

Even then all was not necessarily lost. There was still

room for manœuvre and a chance to find other forms of negotiation through other representatives. Since the symbol of authority had abandoned his responsibilities a new set of ground rules was needed for the bargaining process. The crowd now wanted to administer their own justice to Labbé since the police had betrayed their trust. But it is interesting that although they could have taken Labbé by force at any moment, the crowd still preferred to employ the familiar rituals of negotiations. Even though the commissioner had given up and the officers of the Watch were outnumbered by their attackers, yet the crowd still required the good offices of a mediator.

The man who emerged from the crowd to assume the role was not completely insignificant. Claude-Toussaint Parisis was 'an employee of the Royal Entertainment Stores'. Doubtless he was no more than an ordinary clerk, but he nevertheless wore the King's grand livery with red cloth facings (a fact which was referred to four times during his interrogation at the official inquiry).[19] At the height of the uprising this man seems to have been the only person who could make himself heard by both the rioters whose spokesman he became, and the officers of the Watch whom he advised to give Labbé to the crowd or risk being massacred. The distant authority whose device he wore gave him universal prominence and credibility at the time, although he was later suspected of being in collusion with the rioters. During the official inquiry he was harshly accused of 'having thus established himself as the mediator between a mutinous mob and the law-enforcement officers'. There is no way of knowing whether the dialogue he reported several weeks later in front of the acting magistrate actually took place on the afternoon of 23 May. The first priority for this witness, who was in danger of himself becoming a suspect, was to demonstrate his credibility to the judge. The incredible air of performance and the ostentatious civilities which Parisis deemed necessary for a plausible account suggest that the actual exchange had been strictly formalized in the telling.

The accused answered that in view of the crowd's fury and the consequent risk to the officers of the Watch he was imprudent enough to come forward wearing the grand livery and, having removed his hat to the sergeant, addressed him thus: 'Sergeant, I have just been advised that unless you grant the people satisfaction, they will wrest it from you and hack you to pieces.' The sergeant answered the accused, 'Sir, I thank you and I pray you inform the people that satisfaction will be granted to them.' The witness then made his bow and returned to the crowd informing them, 'The sergeant has just given me his assurance that you will receive satisfaction.' He then returned to his place of work.

Labbé was handed to the crowd, who were at last able to wreak their vengeance on him. The deed was a collective act, carried out publicly, in the street. A final confession was cruelly denied him at the very door of Saint-Roch church where one of the rioters mocked him pitilessly crying, 'There's your confessor!' as he threw a cobblestone at his head. Labbé was no longer able to make his peace with anyone. This time nobody, not even a clerk, could intercede between the victim and his persecutors.

Later that evening the crowd, who had proved impervious to the efforts to disperse them, forced the funeral cortège to retrace the route of failed negotiations and final massacre in full public view. It was a reminder that the crowd had achieved retribution in its own way. Gueulette, the state prosecutor, noted that:

> The corpse was placed on a ladder to be carried to the Basse Geôle. Apparently the crowd demanded that the bearers lift the ladder onto their shoulders so that the poor man who no longer had a human face, could be clearly seen by all. This was done and the cortège was then accompanied by a large group of people who forced the archers to follow the long route through the streets.[20]

The rioters had not quite finished with the authorities, who had up to that point given way before them. When they dragged Labbé's body to Berryer's door, it was more than just the action of an uncontrolled crowd; it was a challenge. They were delivering the servant to the master and in doing so were pointing an accusing finger at Berryer and waiting for his reply. The answer never came. Two days later reaction came from a very different quarter when Parliament took charge of the affair. The new interlocutor was well chosen. By tradition it was the Court which administered the city of Paris in the King's name, and it too favoured a more traditional rule of discipline than that which the new style of police had attempted to enforce. Thus in being appointed to the task the Court was taking a certain revenge of its own. D'Argenson, optimistic for once, was able to write: 'Everyone is very heated in Paris and everywhere else. Parliament has assumed the mantle of a noble lord. It is as though a deposed minister had been reinstated with greater powers than ever. Parliament has become the mediator between the King and the people.'[21]

Only at that point could the revolt reach its conclusion.

4

Truth and Rumour

It is difficult to assess the true facts of the events which took place in 1750. Not that the inquiry was not conducted conscientiously by the police and magistrates; but the whole emphasis was on establishing culpability, particularly that of the rioters, rather than verifying factual detail. For one thing the number of victims of the May riots remains uncertain. The police figure of twenty dead is unverifiable although, on the face of it, it seems excessive. The number of wounded is even more uncertain.[1] But a more serious problem lies in establishing the facts of the abductions. The affair dealt with the sensitive area of police corruption, and this, together with the constant presence of wild rumours and the fact that the inquiry laid more emphasis on the revolt itself than its causes, meant that doubt was often cast on the truth of the abductions. The chroniclers, for instance, were often dubious about the stories, and thirty years after the event Mercier was referring to 'a rumour which may or may not have been true that children were being abducted'. This uncertainty on the part of contemporaries sometimes affected the historians who later drew on their accounts for source material. But there are many documents existing in the archives that dispel any such doubts.

First and foremost there are a number of statements by children and their parents who had experienced police harassment. On Shrove Tuesday, 23 March 1750 Louis Taconnet, who lived in the rue Colombier, went out with three friends after their catechism class. The boys had left the city by the Notre-Dame-des-Champs gate and were playing 'stones' with some tiles they had picked up on the way to the rue de Vaugirard when:

> They were followed by three men who pretended to join their game when a fourth man appeared who seized them, arrested them and put them in a carriage where there were four other men dressed in blue and carrying rifles; when he asked why he was arrested, Taconnet was told that they were only doing it to frighten them. He then asked to be taken to the commissioner and the men asked what good that would do, but when the witness persisted they promised to take him there which they did not do but instead put him in Grand Châtelet prison.[2]

Taconnet was fifteen and a half years old. Jean-François Joly was only nine. He was a cloth worker and lived with his parents in the faubourg Saint-Martin. 'On 1 May he was on his way to collect his little niece to take her home as his mother had told him when he was suddenly seized in the rue Croix-des-Marais.' Jean-François explained 'that he had not been playing, that it was Monsieur Le Blanc who had taken him, that they put him in a carriage where there were twelve others like him and took him to the Grand Châtelet where he spent eleven days'.[3]

Marguerite Ollier was a laundress and the widow of a

journeyman carpenter. Her statement refers to an incident which took place in December 1749 or early 1750
and it conjures up a scene reminiscent of a picture by
Greuze.

> Six months ago at 9 o'clock one evening she was busy
> working at home and her only son of thirteen had just
> gone to bed when three men appeared, one of whom
> wielded a stick and said he was a constable. They said
> they had come on the King's orders, then one of them
> asked her if her son had brought her any linen and
> another one told the boy, 'Get up and get dressed, you
> rascal!' She was in floods of tears and the child got
> dressed and said, 'Don't cry, mother, these gentlemen
> won't harm me.' They took him in the direction of the
> commissioner's residence while she followed holding
> his hand but then he was taken straight to the Châtelet
> without going to the commissioner's at all and he spent
> eight days in prison . . .[4]

These are just three examples of twenty or more
similar testimonies. The individual circumstances differ
but the salient features are the same in each case. The
abduction was effected by surprise, no regard was given
to the children's age or status and the victims' protestations were ignored. Furthermore the arrests were carried out without legal process and were frequently
accompanied by verbal or physical threats.

The children's evidence was, by and large, upheld by
that of the five law enforcement officers who were
interrogated together with the rioters at the inquiry on
26 May.[5] There were two constables, two officers of the
Watch and a police inspector, although the five men
represented in reality only a tiny proportion of the
police operation mounted by the Lieutenant General in

response to the edict of 1749. All five of them admitted to the facts whilst, understandably, trying to minimize their gravity. Some of them had been operating outside their normal sphere of activity and were going beyond their usual prerogative on direct written orders from Berryer, which they had taken great care to preserve and which they now presented to the judges as proof. They had agreed to carry out the unusual duties because 'a man must live'. Besides which, Berryer had put pressure on them and they had been tempted by the bonuses which would considerably increase their meagre income. All of them admitted to having had doubts about the legitimacy if not the legality of the work they had undertaken and all except one of them explained their state of mind.

Sébastien Le Blanc received a brief from Berryer which he returned a month later on 15 May, 'having realized how unhappy the public was with these captures'. Julien Danguisy, a sergeant of the Watch, stated that 'he had not gone looking for the work, it had been presented to him', but that he had been uneasy about possible future consequences and 'had taken care to ensure that his daughter kept lists of all his captures in writing . . . he thought she still had the names in a book.' In fact, of course, Danguisy could just as well have been using the list to claim his bonuses. Danguisy had worked together with an officer of the Watch called Faillon who said that he had accepted the job 'in the hope of eventually gaining better employment which is what Berryer had the goodness to promise him.' However, Faillon found he had 'no stomach for the work' and he chose to give it up. He too kept an account of his captures for the month when he admitted to being involved from 12 March to 16 April, after which his experience of a rather heated confrontation persuaded him to give up the work.

Finally there is the evidence of Inspector Brucelle, whose rank meant that he dealt directly with the Lieutenant General of Police and who had started arresting children long before the November edict. In March 1749 he had received some instructions from Berryer 'which seemed questionable' (these written instructions are in the archives) but which he nevertheless carried out until November when the new edict appeared to clarify the situation somewhat. Brucelle attempted to demonstrate his reluctance by showing himself to have been less than zealous when arresting children. He said 'he had arrested between sixty and eighty whereas he could have arrested three hundred and Monsieur Berryer told him he was not making enough captures'.

The five accused were all laying blame on the Lieutenant General, hoping to gain the magistrate's leniency for themselves. They had guessed that the judges would not be averse to placing ultimate responsibility at Berryer's door. This tactic did achieve the desired result; nevertheless the evidence suggests that Berryer's authority had not been their only motivation. Their detailed accounts to the court bear out the general truth of the victims' and their parents' statements. Danguisy, for instance, explained how he and his men used surprise tactics when making arrests:

> When they learnt that gambling was taking place somewhere, they would send someone dressed as a cook, worker or bourgeois who would pretend to watch the game. When Faillon appeared with the squadron, which always accompanied them lest they be thought to be

arresting beggars, the gamblers would try to disperse
and the 'cooks' would then seize them all including the
individual in charge of the money.

Le Blanc also confirmed that his men worked in
everyday bourgeois clothes 'for greater efficiency'. All
five men confirmed that their orders were to take the
arrested children directly to prison without first going
to the commissioner. They claimed to have warned
parents whenever they could before the children's imprisonment made matters more complicated, but that it
had not always been possible. Besides, they were afraid
of being suspected of making ransom demands on the
families themselves, a fear which was well founded
according to some witnesses.

The evidence of both victims and accused raises questions about the nature of the abductions. Who exactly
were being arrested in 1749 and 1750? The terms used
are ambiguous. The documents refer with lack of precision to 'children' or 'little boys'; this gives no clear
indication of the true ages of those involved. The definitions cover a hazy period from infancy to an adolescence
which was sometimes prolonged into the early twenties
if a boy was still living at home with his parents.
Occasionally, a youth of 14 or 15 was loosely referred to
as a 'little boy'. The broad age range raised a variety of
different issues, particularly from the point of view of
penal responsibility. The legal age of responsibility was
11 or 12 years, and below that age a child was not liable
to a court hearing or imprisonment even if he had been
earning an independent living for some time. The terms
used to describe the victims can therefore be misleading,
and this was the line of defence taken by Hamart, the

only constable to deny all the charges against him. The other accused also stressed the efforts they had made to judge the boys' ages. During one of his rounds of Paris, Le Blanc came across 'several rascals and street urchins who were gambling', on which occasion he simply 'arrested two of the older players and sent the others on their way with a warning'. He took care to note in his diary that the two he had arrested were 16 and 17 years old. Brucelle, despite the orders he had received, 'only arrested young people between 15 and 20 and in any case they were youths so deserving of detention that everyone in the neighbourhood approved of his actions'. However, in the same passage he goes on to admit that 'later, when submitting his report to Berryer, he had the honour to inform him that amongst the groups of gamblers he had come across several very young children and even sons of bourgeois citizens, and Berryer had said: "Good, Brucelle, they are precisely the ones I want arrested." And because of that he had carried on.'

While not providing any precise statistics, the overriding evidence leaves no doubt that alongside the usual contingent of youths, delinquent or otherwise, a fair number of younger children were taken. We have already quoted the evidence of nine-year-old Jean-François Joly. François Copin, eleven years old, was on his way back from delivering a letter on the morning of 16 May when he was stopped near the Place aux Veaux 'by an individual who was a constable and who told him, "Get into the carriage with us and we'll give you something", and they put him in the carriage where there were eight other children including two little girls of five and eight years old'. He and his two fellow victims were saved by the timely intervention of a local soldier of the Guard who recognized him.[6] The little Laporte boy, who was taken while his parents were 'drinking beer' at home, was nine years old. His parents only just managed to save him.[7] A coach driver whose vehicle had been requisitioned by an officer, probably Danguisy, accompanied him on his rounds of the capital on 14 May. In his statement he said that of the six 'young people' arrested in the Place du Carousel and the rue du Roule, there were 'four young 10- or 12-year-olds' and 'one little one who was reclaimed by a footman'. His orders were then to drive to the Capucins.[8] A large number of the victims fell in the crucial 11- to 12-year-old age group, and several children below that age were certainly arrested in Paris.

Age was not the only concern; the boys' social status was another cause of resentment. The public would probably have tolerated without demur a plan to rid Paris of young street urchins, just as they had long supported the expulsion of the capital's vagrants. But the documents reveal that the police did indeed cast their net wider than that, despite their protestations to the contrary. Constable Hamart denied having tracked down anyone outside the usual range of police suspects. Inspector Dumont confirmed the point by citing the example of two 13- and 14-year-old boys on the run who were caught begging and whose parents were not even anxious about their whereabouts before being summoned by the police: 'That is how rumours are spread about the abduction of respectable bourgeois children whereas in fact they are little wastrels on the loose.'[9] These testimonies, however, are unusual and run counter to the version of events suggested by the inquiry as a whole.

No doubt the batch of arrests included some real gamblers and even some persistent offenders like Pierre Barlamant, taken in the Place Vendôme on 20 April and who, at 17, had already been arrested on the same charge the previous year. But the cases most frequently cited involved the sons of craftsmen, merchants or workers who were often already engaged in a trade themselves. Twelve-year-old Nicolas Savoie, arrested on 23 April, was the son of a box-maker in the rue de Buci. Louis Taconnet was a master baker's son. Alexandre Regnault's father was a master pin-maker in the Saint-Paul district and his aunt, who came forward to testify on his behalf, was a fruit merchant. Georges-Jean Bachevilliers, fifteen and a half, was a craftsman who worked with his father, a master button-maker. The young Millard, who was taken in the rue Royale, was the son of a watch-maker. Marie-Madeleine Bizet, who came to claim her son from prison, was married to one of the King's spur-makers. None of these families were members of that *petit bourgeoisie* who were so fiercely proud of their station in society.

Some families also represented a section of the more humble bread-winners such as seamstresses, porters and laundresses. Some of the children were just apprentices, trainee rope-makers or humble clerks. And of course there were a number of the ubiquitous street urchins who made up the dregs of the capital's juvenile population. But wherever they ranked in the Parisian social hierarchy, nearly all the plaintiffs had recognized occupations, and the fact that the boys were arrested while going about their daily business added to their families' indignation. Taconnet had been coming from his catechism class, as had several others. Twelve-year-old François Gautier was still a schoolboy and was taken while running errands for his father. Inspector Brucelle was even accused of taking 'a child who had just been sprinkling holy water over a corpse lying in the doorway'. In general the police operation was seen as particularly scandalous because it disrupted the balance of daily life to which the boys made important contributions. Furthermore, adding insult to injury, the police often used verbal or physical threats or else accompanied the arrests with mocking jibes.

Lieutenant General Berryer's auxiliaries confirmed the evidence. When the magistrates observed that Le Blanc had not only arrested rogues and that 'his book listed many children who had families and who were mostly sons of Parisian artisans', he admitted the fact and asserted that, 'if he had known earlier, he would have released them'. Danguisy's list showed 'that he arrested many children of saddlers, cobblers and shopworkers who were clearly not disreputable'. Faillon justified himself by assuring the judges that if his orders 'had directed him to arrest only one type of person, he would have done so'. The potential financial bonuses doubtless accounted in part for the policemen's lack of discrimination in making their arrests, but Berryer's demands were also a strong determining factor. We have already seen how Brucelle, who answered directly to the Lieutenant General of Police, pin-pointed his guilt most clearly. Brucelle emphasized both the difficulty 'of distinguishing street urchins and disreputable people from other types' and Berryer's willingness and positive encouragement to use excessive measures.

It is important to examine the Lieutenant General's ruthlessness which, in their concern for self-preservation, the accused held responsible for all the brutality and cynicism. In actual fact, however, it would appear that Berryer, in acting as he did, believed that he was falling in with the will of the people as well as pleasing the minister and the Royal Court. When Faillon questioned him on the legality of the operation, he answered that:

> It was acceptable to arrest all children of workers and bourgeois alike caught gambling in the squares and market places along with the other little rascals and vagabonds because . . . several parents had complained to him that their own children were stealing money from them at home to gamble with and that they would be doing these parents a favour by arresting their children and punishing them as a warning to others.[10]

Berryer repeated his reasons before the judges. Was he sincere or merely led astray by his own zeal and desire for his name to be associated with the re-establishment of public order? He probably had received some complaints from parents although the inquiry only produced one witness whose testimony upheld the theory. It is more likely that the policy of indiscriminate arrests arose from the dynamics of police policies which became distorted by their own abusive logic.

The fact remains that young people were arrested in Paris and that their numbers included some whose age, status and behaviour made their arrest inappropriate and unacceptable. It is also clear that this breach of convention led to increased violence. It is impossible to arrive at any precise figures. Danguisy admitted to 27 arrests, although his notebook mentions 46. Le Blanc too registered 46 in just one month. Faillon arrested 45 between mid-March and mid-April. Brucelle's tally was between

60 and 80. Even allowing for the fact that these figures are approximate and that individual lists sometimes overlapped, they still provide only a small fraction of the total since there were many other inspectors, constables, spies and clerks working for Berryer between December 1749 and May 1750. There were probably several hundred abductions carried out at the time. The other question is how many of the victims were vagabonds and how many respectable children. We can never be sure of these figures either. The official inquiry report provides a false picture since the only evidence is from those boys and their parents who had suffered unjustly. Possibly these were in the minority. But the precise figures were far less important than the rumours which the abuses instantly gave rise to.

The Rumour of the Children

In retrospect, the magnitude of the affair's repercussions seems out of proportion to its causes. The parliamentary edict of 1750 gave sudden prominence to high-handed practices, which were, in themselves, nothing new. Berryer was undoubtedly responsible for the harshening of repressive measures towards vagrants, but the process of sudden arrest followed by immediate imprisonment without the due judicial procedure of a commissioner had been commonly practised since the beginning of the eighteenth century, both by the 'new' inspectors and the traditional archers of the Hôpital Général.[11] The same was true for the abuses of power practised by law and prison officers in all their corrupt daily affairs.

The abduction of young boys, if not of children in the
true sense of the word, had been known for over a
century. As early as 1663 the King had ordered the
judicial commissioners of Châtelet to provide information on similar incidents which had already led to street
riots against the archers. Similar events reoccurred in
1645, 1701, 1720, then again during the 1730s.[12] Abductions were always resented, but at least in previous years
the motives underlying the threat to young people had
been widely understood. Apart from the constant concern to maintain public order, there was also the desire
to recruit colonists for the Islands and Louisiana. These
reasons were certainly unpopular with the Parisians, but
they were at least comprehensible and would have been
enough in themselves to explain Berryer's policy. In
fact, during the events of 1750, the population of Mississippi was put forward as a plausible reason for the
arrests both by those involved in the uprising and by
more detached commentators like Barbier and d'Argenson.

However, no precedent or plausible reason was sufficient to answer all the questions raised by the events of
1750. The whole affair remained obscure, intriguing
and shocking, giving rise to endless speculation. Other
reasons were sought to explain the mystery, not only by
the populace who were always assumed to be naïvely
credulous, but by the authorities themselves, who were
also convinced that on this occasion there was some
other cause to be uncovered.

Berryer was the first to try to convince the magistrates, with political hindsight, that rumours had been
deliberately spread in Paris to undermine public order.
One of the witnesses produced by Berryer in support of

his theory described the type of person who had been whipping up the crowd at the time of Labbé's murder. He denounced the presence of

> three young men of about 18 or 20, fairly well dressed and carrying swords, who seemed to be applauding the treatment which had just been meted out to Labbé. As soon as the corpse was at Berryer's door, the same young men reappeared standing quite close to those who were throwing stones, and they were joined there by a fourth young man who was also quite well dressed and aged about 26 or 27.

D'Argenson had also heard that 'these popular disturbances were incited and led by people superior to the general populace.' But he himself was not convinced by the rumours.[13]

Parliament, on the other hand, was less prepared to believe in the existence of a political plot than in the responsibility of agitators, rumour-mongers or layabouts backed by the criminal underworld. They believed that this group made up the greater part of the rioters and it was towards them that they directed their enquiries. The Lieutenant General of Police and the magistrates, however, confined themselves to the essentials from the very first. They knew the form and nature of the abductions and had not much to learn about the reasons behind them. They inclined towards the hypothetical plot idea, less perhaps from their natural inclination to credit such a theory than in an attempt to comprehend the sudden extraordinary importance that the affair had assumed.

Naturally, people were well aware of the current harshening of repressive measures, which they strongly resented, particularly since they were the first to feel the effects of them. The fact that confrontations with Berryer's henchmen had multiplied in recent months was due to this general awareness that the situation was hardening. People were not slow to demonstrate their resentment against the 'new' police force. It was known that the young people arrested were destined for prison or, it was thought, Mississippi, as was evidenced by one mother who believed that her son had already left for America. But even these beliefs did not provide a sufficient explanation for events. There was some other element involved, which defied explanation. Rumour alone could define and elucidate this elusive factor.

All the experts agree that rumour was an intrinsic part of the city's life. Lenoir, who was Lieutenant General of Police at the end of the eighteenth century, developed the theme at length and recalled that even 30 years later, the affair of the child abductions 'is not forgotten by people in this town'. He came to the unoriginal conclusion that rumour was an irrepressible phenomenon which could never be beaten. 'The Parisians were more inclined to believe in false reports and libels circulated clandestinely than in the reports printed and published on government orders.'[14] The persistence of rumour confirmed the social nature of oral communication and was, above all, an expression of the emotion and credulity which formed part of the psychological stereotype of the people at the time. Just like superstition, with which it is often allied, rumour is one form of identifying a collective identity.

In 1750, rumour was certainly rife, or rather a whole series of rumours enclosed within each other like Chinese boxes. This fact alone would account for the rapid

spread of information in this immense city where individuals and families normally functioned within the
limited confines of a parochial, district framework.[15]
Most of the arrests whose details are known to us from
the inquiry's report gave instant rise to large gatherings
of people, and the news of them spread very rapidly
throughout Paris. The initial incident was always a
small and trivial one such as happened several times a
day in the city, yet it was enough to mobilize the crowd
with abnormal speed. Why was this so?

In the first place it was because each incident was
public and yet incomprehensible. Some men, who were
usually in plain clothes, but whose dress and general
demeanour soon became recognizable, questioned boys
in the streets, in the squares or at toll-gates, then,
without any judicial process, carried them off in closed
carriages. Or, worse still, they took the boys from their
homes or followed them into the houses where they had
sought refuge.[16] Marie-Jeanne Fouquet, a fish and herb
merchant in the Bourg-Tibourg market, gave a typical
account of one such episode.

> [She] saw two children taken in the Saint-Jean cemetery
> on Easter Day. One man was holding the youngest
> Regnault boy and an archer was holding another child
> whose female relatives were all in the market at the time
> and who tried to retrieve him. It was Monsieur Dan-
> guisy in charge of the operation, though she only saw
> his hat, and millions of people in the market begged him
> to release the child.[17]

Her whole testimony, including its exaggerated ending,
attests to the affair's strange mixture of the familiar and
the extraordinary which gave rise both to powerful
emotions and a plethora of various commentaries.

The more frequently the abductions occurred, the better they became understood. People learnt to take note of the details and to identify the perpetrators. The methods involved and their likely outcome became more clearly perceived with each incident. But the police operations themselves remained unpredictable and shrouded in secrecy. The rumours being spread by word of mouth retained above all the essential information necessary to identify the victims and the enemy. In this way the outline of a story was created which, whether true or false, was familiar, credible and sufficient in itself to incite reaction. This, for example, was the rumour reported by an anonymous informer concerning the last abduction attempt, which took place on 23 May and which was to cost Labbé his life:

> There is an upholsterer who lives with his wife and daughter near the gates of the Palais Royal. It is said that the man put to death by the crowd . . . had that morning given some money to the upholsterer's daughter to go and buy some cherries and that a woman who had witnessed this warned the mother that the man was a child abductor and that started the rumour which eventually led to the man's murder.[18]

Barbier mentions this rumour, which he himself distrusts, but which he reports as a professional city watcher, referring to a 'widespread public rumour' and using the impersonal form of 'It is said . . .'.

All the testimony indicates that some groups were more inclined to rumour-mongering and gossip than others. Domestic servants in particular created a formidable network of information with their chatter in the streets or at their windows. Women too appeared to be especially prone to gossip. Brucelle always refers to women as the main participants in any incident. Once, he heard them 'yapping' in the market, and on another occasion they made 'such a hullabaloo' that he was forced to release four young urchins he had arrested. It was a group of women whom Lequesne heard muttering before they discovered his hiding place at the beer merchant's in the rue des Nonnains d'Hyères, and it was they who alerted the neighbourhood and ran to fetch the officers of the Watch. Inspector Roussel also indicated the central role played by women. His spies reported 'that the idea that children are still being taken grows daily among the populace, particularly the women'. And again it was the women's powerful network that carried the rumour as far as the suburbs where at Vincennes on 22 May a group of them surrounded two 'child abductors from Paris'.[19]

Moufle d'Angerville, who gave an account of the affair thirty years after the events, ultimately saw the role of women as being the key to the whole 1750 uprising:

A constable, who was greedy for money and hopeful of immunity, took a child planning to demand a ransom from the child's mother for its return. The power of maternal love is legendary. Even in the animal kingdom the mildest female becomes ferocious, wild and completely unrecognizable in defence of her young. The woman in question, far from being intimidated, let her cries ring out throughout the surrounding neighbourhood. Other mothers with similar fears joined her and soon it was no longer a case of one or two children being kidnapped but thousands ... it was the women who started the uprising in the faubourg Saint-Antoine which spread and was then taken up by the men until it eventually reached the centre.[20]

D'Angerville's version of affairs is very subjective and highlights certain factors that he considered to be important. In stressing the prominence of women and referring to a traditional feminine role, he was minimizing the importance of the revolt as a whole. In the history of emotional turmoil, women often took the limelight because they were less vulnerable to the repercussions of police and judicial repression than were the men. D'Angerville was certainly well informed being, for instance, one of the authors who completed Bachaumont's *Mémoires secrets*. It is possible that his insistence on the importance of women also referred to other factors. Indeed much of the evidence reveals the active part played by women beyond involvement in the actual uprisings. They provided hiding places 'for little children afraid of being taken', 'made declarations before the commissioner' and even drew up petitions protesting against the arbitrary arrests and attempted to secure the release of Berryer's prisoners.[21] So women were far more than simply harbingers of rumour. They often took matters into their own hands and expressed themselves in practical ways.

The women's involvement was surely due largely to the fact that the affair concerned children, albeit not necessarily their own. Young people were being taken in full public view in the course of their daily activities and having their honesty called into question. Françoise Linotte explained that: 'The most painful thing was that one of the archers disguised as a cook told her that her son was involved in activities for which he could be hanged (he was one of the infamous bootblacks), which meant that her son was publicly branded as a thief.' On the other hand, Marie-Madeleine Bizet sang the praises of 'a little boy who runs errands in the neighbourhood and does needlework in his spare time. He was abducted and the whole district became involved.' Her account describes a child who was regarded as a paragon by his family and neighbours, which only served to highlight the cruelty of his tormentors.[22] All the mothers were careful to point out to the magistrates the solicitude with which they continued to care for their boys when they were in prison, although the arrest often meant a severe loss of income for the family. Clearly the feminine protest went far beyond the archetypal folklore image of militant shrews up in arms against authority. Nor was their motivation limited to the simple emotional response of motherhood. What the women most strongly resented about the abductions was the disruption of existing social threads. From this point of view it mattered little whether the boys were children in the true sense of the word or indeed whether they were well known or, on the contrary, total strangers. The menace of abductions looming over Paris did more than upset the social balance and network of solidarity; it touched on the very sources of life itself. The child became the potent symbol of a defensive collective identity.

During the middle years of the eighteenth century, a new awareness of the child was gaining expression in several ways. This awareness was taking shape at a level which was quite separate from the moral and pedagogic issues simultaneously appearing in contemporary intellectual literature. It was rooted in a series of events whose repetitive nature transformed them into exemplary, symbolic tales. In a way, this is comparable to what happened with the series of child abductions that took place in France during the 1970s or, ten years later, the murders of elderly women in Paris. Such events usually serve to highlight areas of anxiety in a given society. The anecdotes abounded, not only in the predictable pages of the chroniclers, but in the broadsheets and street gossip gleaned by the police.

For examples of this, it is enough to look to Barbier who was always sensitive to current feelings. As early as 1734 he turned his attention to a scandal which was affecting the whole of Paris: 'Fifteen or sixteen small children's corpses have appeared at the Châtelet morgue. One of them was three years old and the others were younger, some new-born. The sight drew a large crowd and instilled general fear.' Bewilderment was widespread. Were they abandoned children? Was it a mass murder? Eventually it was revealed that a doctor had assembled the little corpses, 'for anatomical studies'. The affair dragged on, bringing an unpleasant atmosphere of suspicion in its wake, which worried Barbier. Even several months later, 'the people considered taking revenge for such a cruel spectacle...'.

In March 1749 an incident occurred with a different scenario but similar response. Some 40 young girls from the Halles district were seized with vomiting and convulsions during the catechism class they were attending in preparation for their first communion. This happened every two days, 'which seemed extraordinary'. 'Someone noticed that an old beggar woman had approached the girls, pulled a handkerchief out of her pocket and shaken it. Those little girls who had not been taken ill said that they had seen the same woman on Friday and that she was a witch and a poisoner. The whole neighbourhood was thrown into alarm.' Anxiety must have spread rapidly throughout the whole town, since the next day 'a beggar woman was seen climbing the steps in Saint-Sauveur parish, and a little girl cried out that she was the witch-poisoner of Saint-Eustache. The woman was instantly surrounded by 200 men and women.' It was then discovered that the noxious fumes emanating from the *Innocents* charnel house were responsible for the children's sickness, but by then the seeds of suspicion had already been sown.

From horror stories we turn to a fairy story. In 1749 the Dauphin and Dauphine provided a tale to add to the list. The couple had no children of their own and they had both publicly declared their desire to adopt and raise a child. The princess wanted a boy whereas the prince preferred a little girl. One day they saw from their window a poor carpenter's wife in the gardens of Versailles who was burdened with five little children, four or five years old, who were not all her own. 'There's what I want' said the prince, who had set his heart on a 'very dirty, muddy little girl'. The child was cleaned and dressed and brought before her benefactor. 'Here was a new distraction. The Dauphin said he would take care of her, he wanted her to be well educated and he would have a genealogy drawn up for her because it was not the first time that people of quality had fallen on hard times. He named her Mademoiselle de Tourneville.' Then the prince sent his find to the convent at Saint-Germain-en-Laye. Barbier concludes this pretty tale of royal kidnap by predicting every future blessing for the child. Nevertheless it was in its own way simply another abduction.

Another singular affair which set tongues wagging in Paris during the last days of 1749 happened around Christmas when a young girl, 'of 17 or 18, quite pretty and well dressed', appeared at Saint-Etienne-du-Mont during mass. She seemed not to know what she was doing and did not know what a mass was, nor a priest nor a church. When questioned she eventually told her story and said 'that she had been incarcerated in a house all her life and that one day she had happened to find the door open and had made her escape.' The vicar and commissioner were alerted and she proceeded to furnish further details of her life. She and her sister had been imprisoned by their father, 'who sometimes mistreated her'. She explained 'that she had never seen or spoken to a man apart from the gardener whom she saw from her window. Her father shared a bed with her elder sister and she had heard him say that he would kill her sister and then marry her.' Altogether she spun a fine tale of innocence such as the Age of Enlightenment delighted in. Naturally, the girl could remember having been abducted at the age of four. It took a week to discover that this heroine who had captivated the hearts of Parisians was an imposter. She was a working man's daughter who had possibly hoped to gain some nobleman's favour. She was to end up in the convent of the penitents at Saumur.

Apart from these dramatic stories, there are the usual run of the mill accounts of violence towards children, which the chronicler duly noted. In June, after the riots, one woman was condemned to be whipped and branded for attracting a five-year-old boy and stealing his ragged clothes. The arrest was loudly broadcast in the streets, 'so as to keep the people abreast of the affairs involving children although she had nothing really to do with that'. In July, a procuress called Mayon received the same punishment, 'for having abducted and attempted to debauch a ten-year-old girl' who had been destined for a noble client. These incidents are trivial when taken in isolation, and even as a whole they do not tell a unique story but are simply variations on a number of common themes. Each episode features a child (a definition which in itself became reinterpreted) who is submitted, for good or evil, to the will of adults seeking to use him or her for their own ends. There is no doubt, as Barbier himself suggests, that each of these episodes created connections and echoed each other in ways which gave rise to new modes of thought.[23]

The rumours not only took hold everywhere but, having taken hold, were tenacious. Commenting on the events at Saint-Eustache, the chronicler observed that 'This affair which had so far confined itself to the populace soon became a topic of conversation in all the homes in Paris on a more serious level.' Eventually even the King, Madame de Pompadour and the Court became implicated. And when the innocent girl of Saint-Etienne-du-Mont was exposed as a fake, Barbier noted that people from all walks of life came to visit and question her, including people of quality, and that the affair became a talking point, 'throughout almost the whole of Paris'. In fact one of Barbier's persistent themes is that such items of news or interest gradually transcended social barriers and fed on beliefs which were common to people at all levels of society. A good example of this is demonstrated by the last and most serious of the rumours that were circulating in 1750.

A Tale of Blood

We return to Barbier: 'It has been put about that the reason behind these child abductions was that there was a leprous prince whose cure required one or more baths of human blood, and since there is no purer blood than that of children, these were being taken to be bled from all four limbs, then sacrificed. The people are even more outraged by this.' However, he no sooner mentions the rumour than he dismisses it: 'No one knows where such stories came from. This cure was propounded in the time of the Emperor Constantine who did not, himself, wish to make use of it. But we have no leprous prince here and, even if we did, we would never resort to such a cruel remedy.'

On 26 May, d'Argenson tells a similar story but he implicates the monarch: 'It is being rumoured that the King is a leper and is taking blood baths like a latter-day Herod.' Two days later the Marquise de Pompadour wrote to her brother Abel Poisson, Marquis de Van-dières: 'Speaking of lunacy, you must have heard about the Parisians . I don't think there can be anything so stupid as to believe that people want to bleed their children to bathe a leper prince. I am ashamed to say I thought them less cretinous.'

Many years later the glazier Ménétra, who had been a child in 1750, took up the same story in a different version: 'There was a rumour running around at that time that they were taking young boys and bleeding them and they were never seen again, and that their blood was being used to bathe a princess suffering from an illness which could only be cured by human blood.'[24]

Prince, princess or king, the story is basically the same. However, it is only mentioned specifically by those four contemporaries of the abduction scandal. In later texts, on the other hand, the story reappears with other variations. Mercier mentions it only to dismiss it.

Moufle d'Angerville quotes it without specifying the noble patient's name or sex. In his papers Lenoir, the Lieutenant General of Police, talks of a 'young, sick prince of the Royal House'. At the beginning of the nineteenth century Peuchet, an outstanding expert, takes up the story in his *Mémoires tirés des archives de la police*, for which he must have found information that we have not met with. In his version it was the King's health which, to Parisian minds, was the motive for the abductions.[25]

There is only one conclusion to be drawn from such evidence: that alongside the other more straightforward and less alarming explanations running through the streets of the capital, the blood bath rumour also took hold, though to what extent we shall never know for sure. The fact that we found no trace of the story in the official judicial inquiry is hardly surprising. It would be difficult to imagine the accused, the witnesses, the police and least of all the magistrates being willing to touch, albeit with kid gloves, a rumour amounting to *lèse-majesté*. The relative silence of official sources proves nothing, particularly since the story does not appear only once in isolation but is one of a short series of reappearances suggesting that it is one of those familiar narratives, a model fable all ready for use.

In 1733 a similar rumour about a supposed illness of the Dauphin's had spread without, it seems, taking firm hold in people's minds. And in 1749 a Russian prince visiting Paris had apparently boasted that he knew the secret of a 'cure for frightful leprosy'. Bombarded with questions, he eventually confided in a few important persons. The incident is recounted by Peuchet: 'The root of the cure lay in the transfusion of young blood.

First, one bled the victims white, then one replenished the diseased veins with the liquid from the healthy veins of the children who thus perished.' Peuchet, who retrospectively loathed the ruling classes of the Ancien Régime, even maintains that someone who had been party to this confidence passed it on to Louis XV.

Twenty years later, the theme resurfaces at Lyons in a new version. The House of the Oratorians was taken by storm when the crowds accused the priests of harbouring a one-armed prince; 'and every evening near the college they catch a child and cut off one of its arms to measure against this so-called prince'. Should we regard this lunacy as proof of the 'stupid credulity of the populace' or perhaps as evidence of a retaliatory plot organized by the Jesuits then in exile? Finally, here is the same story once again but this time reversed: in 1762, a pastry-cook of Mantes who had just given birth was offered a sack of gold and a sack of silver by two strangers because 'they needed a child born that day, that the child should be a girl and the mother have borne only girls, their plan being to cause the King's death within the month using the brain and marrow of the infant'. Apart from the money, they also promised to give her another child.[26]

The theme is surely too persistent to be without significance. Naturally, the testimonies do not mean that these barbarous practices actually existed, nor do they even prove that the rumour-mongers believed their own stories. There is a deeper, unspoken truth seeking to take shape and substance by means of the power of rumour, as it had already done in the actions of the rioters. First, where did the rumours come from? Most people who have recorded them attribute them to the credulity of the populace, which was sufficient to engender its own horrors. A small number of others favour the theory of a conspiracy deliberately conducted to instil fear. In the nineteenth century, Capefigue, an historian of Louis XV's reign and himself a rationalist ill disposed to take these 'atrocious ideas' seriously, preferred to believe that Protestant pamphlets from England and Holland were responsible for calculatedly planting these appalling rumours. He does not expand on this theory and we have found no trace of evidence to support it.[27] On this occasion the documents provide no answers and we must look to the rumour itself for its reasons.

The rumour existed on two levels, which need to be clearly distinguished. First, there was the comparison of the abductions to the Massacre of the Innocents, which is an aspect widely borne out by the testimony. The riotous women whom Inspector Roussel observed and heard on his journey to Vincennes spoke in those terms. One of the women 'cried out at the top of her voice that it was like living in the reign of King Herod'. The name recurs several times and was used by the King himself, who expostulated against 'the wicked people who are calling me a Herod'.[28] The biblical reference is hardly surprising in a town where Jansenist preaching had been rife for a quarter of a century and permeated even the humblest levels of society. After all, actual events merely fulfilled the promises of scripture. The lawyer Le Paige, who was a great archivist on the Paris convulsionnaries, commented on the events of 1750 in a letter. In prophetic tones, he claims that the events are the dawn of an apocalypse to be prepared for: 'What father or mother could be so hard-hearted as to allow themselves to be robbed of the children which God gave them? Yet we will witness many others. That which is taking place now is nothing compared with what is yet to come.' He goes on to predict that 'streams of blood will flow; we have already seen the rivers stained with it . . . '.[29]

Such prophecies of bloodshed must have been repeated several times in sermons or during the cruel rituals of the *Secouristes*, who by words, gestures and self-inflicted sufferings, ceaselessly declared the strength of their cause and the monarch's betrayal of the sacred mission entrusted to him by his people. The parallel with Herod had one crucial outcome in that it placed the King himself firmly at the centre of the rumour.

The other important aspect of the rumour is the mention of blood baths for a leprous prince, which is an ancient story drawing on a complex web of allusions.[30] Firstly, there was the fairly widespread belief that equated leprosy with a state of sin. This belief seems to have been particularly strong in Middle Eastern civilizations and is consistently dwelled on in the Bible. The opposition of purity and impurity, stated for example in Leviticus (13, i–vii), is wedded to the theory that separates those who bow to the will of God from those who sin against Him. Leprosy was the punishment meted out to Moses' sister Miriam for slandering her brother, also to Ozias, one of the kings of Judah, who tried to usurp priestly powers, and to Gehazi when, in his greed, he profaned the holy name. Leprosy was the mark of sin, and the rabbinical tradition gave increasing credence to this symbolic correlation. The Christian tradition did likewise and drew on Jesus' cure of lepers to promise the spiritual health of the world. From the early Christian Fathers to the medieval theologians, the spiritual diagnosis gained importance over the physical effects of the disease since, as was written in a late-twelfth-century 'Codex of Sins': 'Everyone in a state of mortal sin is a spiritual leper.'

The number of potential lepers grew accordingly as both Jewish and Christian commentators combed Holy Writ in search of support for the theory. David, who forced Bathsheba into adultery and had her husband murdered so that he could marry her, was struck down amongst his people (Samuel 11, xi–xii). Herod, who married his brother's wife (Mark 6, xvii–xviii), was also punished. Both were kings and throughout the Judaeo–Christian tradition leprosy figures as the royal disease *par excellence*. Constantine, persecutor of Christians, was struck down until his conversion brought him divine cure. Both Richard Cœur-de-Lion and Saint Louis were apparently threatened with the disease although it appears to have been more a case of spiritual diagnosis, which the saintly King Louis told Joinville was worse than the disease itself. The higher the rank of the sinner, the more terrible his chastisement. The disease was particularly a threat to those monarchs who had failed to obey God's commandments or had not made heartfelt conversions. One of the last manifestations of the tradition was Louis XI who, although he did not actually have leprosy, was a bad, cruel king and also a very sick man. His story is told in *Histoire de France* written by Louis XIV's Jesuit historian Father Daniel (published initially in 1696 although it ran to 13 editions until 1755). Daniel tells how King Louis XI tried to stem his body's deterioration by drinking 'blood taken from several children, which he hoped would cure the bitterness of his own blood and restore him to his former vigour'.[31]

The disease had a cure though it is always spoken with horror: human blood. According to the theory of the humours, leprosy in all its forms was linked with bad blood that was hot and humid.[32] Therefore it was necessary to fight the disease with cold, pure blood, such as that of a virgin or child, in which the leper had to bathe. There are numerous instances ever since Pliny first described the remedy, which was used in ancient Egypt to cure elephantiasis. It was the blood of children which was recommended by the doctors (Jewish of course) who attended King Richard and Saint Louis. Apparently the cure was used successfully by Averroes, who mistakenly believed he had leprosy. A virgin's blood was offered as cure to the poor Knight Heinrich by Hartmann von Aue in a late-twelfth-century German poem. Again, a virgin's blood was supposed to cure the leprous chatelaine encountered by Sir Galahad and Sir Percival in certain versions of the Holy Grail. The theme, which was systematically collected by the Grimm brothers at the beginning of the nineteenth century, reappears in folkloric, academic, clerical and secular literature.[33] The legend of Constantine is the most powerful example and the one most often referred to. Punished by leprosy for his sins, the pagan emperor was prescribed a bath of children's blood but, just as the children were about to be sacrificed, he opened his heart to God who instantly cured him and offered him spiritual salvation. Thus, blood was the remedy but the cure lay in refusing it.

Naturally, most of these historical or legendary references, of which there exist many more, were not acces-

sible to the people involved in the riots. Most of the
stories belong to an intellectual tradition, and the most
educated witnesses, such as Barbier and Mercier, seem
to have been mostly familiar with the story of Constantine, though some also mention the legend of Louis XI.
We are unable to verify which stories were circulating
by word of mouth, with the notable exceptions of those
taken from scripture. The constant evocation of King
Herod indicates that these examples from scripture were
probably important in paving the way to interpreting
'signs' and to identifying the sins of the world.
However, the power of rumour meant that a whole
hotchpotch of culture was in circulation in Paris, made
up of snatches of knowledge, truths and half-truths,
including a whole mixture of allusions which were
called upon according to the needs of the moment. We
can only make assumptions about this conglomeration
of ideas, but the scenario is plausible. What was it then
that was being expressed?

Leprosy was essentially a disease of the soul. It struck
those who, out of pride or lack of faith, did not truly
submit to the divine will as had happened to Constantine long ago. It was also a sickness of the spirit, falling
under the zodiacal sign of Saturn – like melancholy,
with which it was often associated. Like the melancho-
lic, the leper was prone to fits of anguish and depress-
ion. He yielded easily to temper and caprice. He was
unable to resist his desires and his sexual appetite was
limitless. There was one man in France in 1750 who
answered to this description, a man who constantly
postponed his true conversion although it was
announced from month to month, a man who was
bored by everything and appeared to be in the grip of a

strange lassitude for life, a man who allowed himself to be ruled by his most base appetites to the point where he abandoned his duty and the fulfilment of his destiny. Rumour had unwittingly revealed its object and the pieces of the puzzle began to fall into place. Here then was the unnamed man who stood revealed by the tales of blood. It was not a prince, nor even the Dauphin, but Louis himself who was the latter-day Herod.

5

The Unloved

The inquiry directed by Councillor Severt lasted two months, from 27 May to 28 July 1750, and was conducted in a responsible manner. The judge examined some 30 cases including those of the five law enforcement officers. He also gathered evidence from 56 witnesses before 11 June and a further 169 in the weeks after that date. During the whole length of the inquiry, rumours continued to run unabated because, although the legal proceedings were in full flow, they were being conducted in closed court. The whole city was on edge waiting for the decision that they hoped would bring them justice. Towards the middle of July, when the case appeared to be completed, Parliament decided to defer judgement for a fortnight. Doubtless the reason for this was that they feared popular reaction, but the delay only served to heighten the tension. On 1 August, the judgement was finally published.

The inquiry tacitly acknowledged the existence of police abuse since Berryer's methods were thenceforth forbidden. The judges also decreed that any person arrested by officers of the Watch or short-robed constables should immediately be taken to the nearest commissioner, who would then be permitted to examine the evidence and question the suspect and witnesses at leisure before initiating legal proceedings or deciding on an appropriate course of action in each case. There was nothing innovative in this: it was simply a return to standard procedure. Nevertheless it was an admission that those who had protested against Berryer's methods had been justified, although responsibility was not explicitly ascribed to the Lieutenant of Police. However, the penalties imposed by the judges indicate that the child abductions were not their main concern; the priority was to punish public insurrection against authority. This is amply demonstrated by the imbalance of the penalties meted out. The constables Le Blanc and Brucelle and the officers of the Watch Danguisy and Faillon were sentenced to a merely symbolic punishment. After having been 'reprimanded . . . on their knees' in the Great Hall of Parliament, they were each to pay a fine of three livres, 'to be donated to the prisoners' food fund at the Palais Conciergerie'. This penalty, which did at least have the merit of acknowledging the men's guilt, might have been sufficient to appease the populace had it not been offset by the severity of the sentence delivered to the three rioters: they were condemned to the gallows. The court obviously foresaw that the judgement would not be well received since it was delivered under heavy police and military guard.

D'Argenson commented sarcastically, 'The mountain has brought forth a molehill. Parliament has worked long and hard on the child abduction inquiry, and the whole mammoth undertaking has resulted in the sentencing of one child whom no one will dare to hang, and two constables who will carry the blame.'[1]

D'Argenson was wrong on one point. The youngest of
those condemned to the gallows was only 16 years old,
but he was indeed to be hanged. Charles-François
Urbain was a young delinquent who had already spent
time in Bicêtre prison. He was 'known for roaming
around at nights and not coming home before three in
the morning . . . he is always laden with snuff boxes and
gold watches which he could only have acquired by
theft.'[2] Urbain claimed to work for his father, a second-
hand clothes dealer in Saint-Germain for whom he
bought and sold rags and bric-à-brac, which he sometimes pilfered. His notoriety in the neighbourhood
meant that he had been easily recognized during the
disturbances of 22 May in the rue de la Calandre, where
he was apparently planning to burn down Commissioner Delafosse's residence. He was identified again in
the abortive attempt to steal weapons from the shops on
the Pont Saint-Michel. The crimes he was accused of
were certainly serious, but the fact is that he was
primarily paying for his reputation, which nobody tried
to defend. He was paying also for his aggressive and
possibly over-frank habits of speech. To Marie-
Charlotte Duval, the wife of a sergeant at whom he had
thrown stones, Urbain declared defiantly that the police
were powerless against the uprising and that 'you are
not hanged for killing a constable, you are not even
whipped or branded, you just have to pay fifty francs,
the price of a post-horse'.[3] This aggressive, subversive
speech would have done more to invoke the magistrates' full severity than anything he had actually done.

The other two condemned men were less colourful
characters. Jean-Baptiste Charvat was a 24-year-old
porter who had come to the capital from Savoie, where

he had left his family. He was accused of having been present at several of the disturbances on 16 May but he denied everything, which probably served to strengthen the case against him. Jean–Baptiste Lebeau was also 24 and a coal porter, an occupation which was generally considered to be prone to trouble-making. He was accused of having taken part in the violence, of having roused the crowd against the guards and of having broken the leg of an archer who had struck him. His case was further complicated by the fact that he himself had been a soldier of the guard for nearly a year, and his file is the only one to go into any real depth.[4]

Clearly Parliament wanted to make a few examples by choosing Lebeau and his two companions in misfortune from a group of several possible scapegoats among the floating population of men and boys who were scratching a living in the city. Certainly the magistrates hoped to intimidate those involved in the rebellion by the severity of these sentences, but they tempered their harshness somewhat with discretion. All the other accused were released and, pointedly, none of those who had taken part in the events of 23 May were detained. That day had seen the culmination of the rioters' anger against the police and had produced many witnesses before the court, but they nevertheless decided to close the file on this most contentious episode. The question was – would this prudent decision be enough to quell any further unrest?

There were immediate rumbles of dissatisfaction with the sentences. For two days people waited in vain for a gesture of clemency from Versailles, which would have put things right. The executions took place in the Place Grève on 3 August in the presence of a large number of troops. When the hour came, the crowd began to rebel and tried unsuccessfully to save the condemned men. The executions had been firmly decided upon to show who was in charge of public order in the town. Barbier confirms this fact unequivocally:

> When the coal porter had mounted the scaffold, all the people in the square cried for mercy whereupon the executioner stopped and allowed the condemned man to climb down a few rungs. At this, the other two men made a small gesture of hope. But there was to be no mercy. At that point the Watch came forward, both mounted and on foot, with bayonets fixed, and went round the square pushing people back, wounding some in the process and pushing several people on top of one another. The execution was carried out. The crowd in the Place Grève were so frightened to find themselves surrounded by armed soldiers that they escaped in fear and confusion all along the Le Peletier and Feraille quays to the other end of the Pont Neuf which only shows that with a modicum of discipline, the people of Paris are easily controlled.[5]

Order was then restored but the affair was not finally laid to rest. D'Argenson and Barbier both spoke of the 'consternation . . . not only among humble people but also among respectable citizens' after the denouement. The sentences were certainly unpopular. The general feeling was that Parliament could not simultaneously acknowledge the truth behind the abductions and deliver such light sentences to the perpetrators, and that they must therefore have tacitly accepted the suppression of the most damning evidence. Conversely, by the same logic, the executed men must have been innocent. Barbier, although he feared violent popular reaction, still declared that 'these executions bring no dishonour to the families of the men hanged'.[6] A few days later, the coal merchants guild had masses said for the soul of Lebeau and manifested their solidarity in groups despite the surveillance of police spies.[7] The police force was suspect and Parliament had effectively discredited itself. But there was one other figure who gradually came to assume some of the guilt during those weeks of mourning. This figure, whose name had so far only been mentioned to be exonerated of all responsibility in the affair, was now brought to the forefront. During the summer of 1750, d'Argenson discovered with great delight that the people no longer loved their King.

Although d'Argenson claimed to have been the first to discover the people's disillusionment with the King, in fact it had been whispered from a long way off. In the introduction to his *Histoire de la Révolution Française*, Michelet dates this emotional about-turn to the middle of the century: 'The King – this idol, this god – became an object of horror. The axiom of the divine right of kings perished forever.' While not being quite as emphatic as Michelet, many historians agree that the emotion that swept the kingdom in 1744, when the King was ill at Metz, represented the last flowering of the people's affection for their 'Well-beloved'. However, in reality the grumblings of discontent had started long before that.

No sooner had the first flush of warmth that greeted the start of Louis's reign, his youth and his marriage faded, than the whispers against him and his entourage began. It seemed as though the eventful intervening phase of the Regency had blotted out the memory of

Louis XIV's last oppressive years, and his great-grandson was now compared with the Sun-King in his youth – a comparison in which the present King invariably came off unfavourably. Louis XV was criticized for his weakness of character and particularly for the lazy side of his nature, referred to as his 'idleness'. The word frequently appears in the reports compiled by the police to gauge public feeling. Fleury was even accused of encouraging his master's dissolute tastes the better to secure his own authority. The young King appeared to be incapable of greatness: 'History will not relate that he battled with all the nations of Europe like his great-grandsire, but that he only waged war on deer.'[8]

Louis seemed to be interested in nothing but the pleasures of a private individual. Attentive only to the gratification of his own desires, he did not even perform the gestures traditionally associated with the role of the sovereign. He refused his royal touch to people suffering from scrofula and very soon ceased to take Easter communion. He dissociated himself from the exiguous, symbolic rituals which formed the tenuous link of consensus between the King of France and his people, and which Louis affected to ignore. When the Queen came to Paris in 1728 to pray before the holy relics of Sainte Geneviève for the birth of a Dauphin, people were shocked at the immodesty of her apparel. 'People said that she might as well . . . have stayed at Versailles . . . that she should at least have approached the churches on foot as the late Queen and Louis XIV always did when they came.' There were also complaints about the meagreness of the alms thrown to the poor and about 'the King's fondness for money'. In the same year, during celebrations held at Versailles, on the occasion of

one of his many recoveries, the King left the fishwives
of Les Halles, who had come to pay their customary
respects, standing at the door of his apartments. When
the women got back to Paris they recalled that 'the late
King Louis XIV had always paid them the honour of
bidding them enter'.[9]

Louis was not only idle and selfish but soon came
under attack for his cruel indifference to suffering. A
story was told of one of his Swiss Guards, convicted of
raping a nine-year-old girl who had died as a result.
Louis contented himself with dismissing the man from
his service and refused to pay any attention to the
petition presented by the little girl's father.[10] There was
talk of the harshness with which he treated his own
children and others close to him. 'Some even say that
the King has changed beyond all recognition and that
the older he gets, the more irrascible he becomes. Apparently not even the princes of the blood may approach
him now.'[11] This regal inaccessibility was not the lofty
sovereignty of a Louis XIV but the capricious whim of a
weak, immature man. Did anything touch his sensibili-
ties? 'They talk of the King's indifference to life and say
that he has no emotions, not even a noble inclination
towards goodness, and he even delights in making it
clear to anyone near him that his only satisfaction is in
despising them.'[12]

Those are just a few examples of the remarks against
Louis gathered in the streets of Paris by police spies in
the early years of the reign. Contrary to what has often
been stated, the hostility did not come solely from
Court circles and an aristocracy frustrated in its political
ambitions. The informers had heard these opinions expressed in the streets, in taverns, in church doorways

and in market places. Nor was it a case of momentary resentment but of an ever increasing body of discontent. Month by month the details built up in the police reports presented the image of an unpopular, 'idle' King.

During the 1740s, the discontented grumbling against Louis changed in its nature and extent.[13] His defects of character had become more intransigent and his public behaviour shocking. At the beginning of the 1730s, Louis embarked on his long series of affairs. He was not particularly blamed for neglecting the Queen in favour of his mistresses – after all his great-grandfather had done as much and equally publicly – but rather for his abuse of royal virility. He was said to be ruled by his senses to the point where he flouted the most fundamental conventions. His first three mistresses, for instance, were three sisters, who followed each other in succession and all died very young. Their deaths were seen by some as judgement for the crime of incest levelled against the King. His unbridled sensuality even led to the suspicion 'that he had a taste for men and that his bodyguards were chosen from amongst his favourites'. There were complaints 'that the King had no ambition to be anything but idle and that at his age he should begin to take charge of the reign himself'.[14] There was also resentment at the way in which the royal mistresses played an increasingly important part in affairs of state. The arrival of 'La Pompadour' on the scene in 1745 served to focus this resentment. The marquise's political role, the favours she obtained for her family and friends and her known links with the world of finance were all further proofs of the idleness of a king who refused to govern properly. She was accused of making a personal fortune by speculating in wheat; and in the famine plot persuasion – a rumour which was repeated throughout the century – she was naturally implicated. The sovereign himself was, at that point, spared from imputation in the affair, but the woman who appeared to be ruling in his place was openly suspected.[15] The royal favourite was the target for an avalanche of scurrilous libels, songs and posters, some of which occasionally reached Louis. Barbier noted in June 1749: 'They say that three weeks ago some appalling verses about the King appeared; some people say they told his life story. A rigorous search is being carried out for the authors.'[16]

During these years, the mounting criticism took on an overtly political tone and found some powerful voices. The Jansenist crisis came to a head towards the middle of the century and formed the core of violently expressed public opinion, which called into question not only the King as an individual but the whole basis of the monarchy. These views were circulated in written handbills, from the pulpits of Paris and by an underground press dominated by the *Nouvelles Ecclésiastiques*.[17] For 20 years accusations against an unjust and impious king had been penetrating the consciousness of Parisians of all classes. Sometimes the complaints were uttered in prophetic, apocalyptic tones, and at other times they took the form of specific threats, such as the invective launched by one convulsionary in 1750: 'Unclean monarch, your days are numbered! You will perish beneath your sceptre and both you and your courtesan will be struck down with tragic death.'[18] The previous year, a poem had been in circulation which opened with the line: 'Arise, spirits of Ravaillac!' The King, having heard the poem, said, 'I see I am destined to die like Henri IV.'[19]

There is no doubt that, besides the oracular declarations whose true importance was finally realized after Damiens's attempted assassination of the King in 1757, the Jansenist struggle gave rise to what must already be called a body of public opinion.[20] It mattered little whether the issues which engaged the public's attention concerned religion, politics or general morals; on the contrary, the very lack of a clear division between these issues lent strength to the *mauvais discours* and its rapid circulation by word of mouth. The same voice of dissension was used for a variety of conflicts. The same rhetorical conviction served to express the demands of Parliament, the protests of a clergy anxious to protect its privileges and the fury of a populace crippled by taxes or threatened with hunger.

In the space of just a few years a climate of enmity became established. The atmosphere was so tangible that a journalist employed by the police reported the indifference which greeted the King's return to the capital in November 1748:

> The Parisians did not display as much joy as was expected; only the royal coaches shouted 'Long live the King!' and no one said a word from the windows. One thing is certain, that we were at the Tuileries at 11 o'clock at night and there was nobody left in the palace or on the streets. It was just as though the King were not there. No one gathered on the pavements during the night apart from a few wine-befuddled drunks.[21]

The antagonism between King and city was mutual. D'Argenson noted the increasing signs of disaffection with delight. The people were murmuring against Louis and Louis knew it. The police sent their spies out onto the streets of the capital: this only exacerbated the mood of defiance, and the general hostility was reported to the King. The chronicler understood what was happening and noted that the King 'shows . . . that he does not love his good city of Paris. I do not know why unless it is because of the Police Lieutenant's constant reports of Parisians speaking ill of His Majesty, composing scurrilous songs and muttering all manner of complaints against the reign.'[22] The echoing whispers only served to widen the gap between King and city. Louis no longer liked coming to Paris, and people noted disapprovingly that at the behest of 'La Pompadour' he had chosen to increase the number of royal residences all around the periphery of the capital he had abandoned. The expense was resented, but it was also primarily seen as an admission of his rupture with Paris. 'You visit Choisy and Crécy, why not come to Saint-Denis?' was the taunting rhyme.*

Under the circumstances, the expression of hostility during the uprising of May 1750 seems surprisingly restrained. The main target for the threats and insults was the police, and the King himself was rarely mentioned. Marguerite Benoist, widow of a spur-maker and herself a clothes merchant, came across a certain Boucher holding forth to everyone in a tavern in the rue Montmartre that 'Berryer and the Lieutenant for Crime were both jackasses and that if things went on much longer . . . The fishwives of Les Halles would be likely to go and grab the King by his hair.'[23] Inspector Roussel, who collected what information he could gather on the days after the revolt, reported the blusterings of a fruit merchant, who apparently said 'that it would be a

---

*The royal tombs were at Saint-Denis.

good idea to attack the two Lieutenants of Crime and Police and then go to Versailles and dethrone the King'.[24] On 13 May, Antoine Severt, the former robber turned police informer for Inspector Poussot, overheard someone in a tavern near the Place des Victoires say that 'our women of Les Halles will all get together and go to Versailles to dethrone the King and tear his eyes out, then they will come back to Paris and kill the Lieutenants of Police and Crime . . .'.[25]

It is important not to read too much into these seditious declarations, no matter how tempting it is to hear echoes of those other women who were to march on Versailles on 5 October 1789. No doubt there were other similar views expressed during the days of the revolt, but they did not represent the sentiments that were uppermost in the general voice of protest at the time. If they had been able to, the police would certainly have reported many more examples of anti–royalist feeling, as they would have been only too happy to deflect the public's aggression from themselves and redirect it towards the sovereign.

It was not the institution of monarchy that was threatened by the crowd's anger against the child abductors, but the person of Louis himself and his warped interpretation of traditionally sovereign qualities. This was no mighty king but one who refused to go to war unless it be against his own people. Louis was said to be 'sick of work; he lets a woman take the reins of government'. He could not even tackle the symbolic and moral reconquest of his own kingdom by undertaking a grand tour of the provinces, as had been suggested to him.[26] No glorious king either, this languid man who was as flaccid as a woman and to whom everything was tedious, who trailed his melancholy from one château to another and who attempted to live like a private person on the very public stage that was Versailles. Nor was he a bounteous king, though he 'no longer knew what to do with all his money'. He was a spendthrift without generosity and he squeezed his subjects for every penny while haggling over alms giving. Most crucially, Louis as king was no longer a symbol of life. He had failed to root his royal charisma in the mystery of the Eucharist; he would not exercise his traditional healing powers; and he was accompanied always by misfortune and death. The father no longer had any love for his children and was feeding on their life-blood. We can never know for sure how many people believed that the latter-day Herod was massacring the innocents to regenerate his own degenerate blood, but the number hardly matters. For those who cared to hear, the story was abroad. The King was a true king no longer.

Yet, in spite of everything, the revolt was no revolution. There was no immediate aftermath to the events of 1750 although, seven years later, Damiens appeared not to have forgotten them.[27] The uprising was merely an important milestone on the road of antagonism which distanced the sovereign from his people throughout those years. Barbier, with detachment, and d'Argenson, with malicious animation, both told the story of this 'extraordinary antipathy'. Louis XV spoke openly of the hostility: 'Well then, he said, why should I show myself to the wicked populace who call me a Herod?' To punish the Parisians, being perhaps also mindful of his own security, he decided not to travel through the capital again. When, in June, he wanted to go from

Versailles to Compiègne, he had a road built through
the Bois de Boulogne which became known as 'le
chemin de la révolte' [the path of the revolt].[28]

The Parisians' response was more subtle in its way.
Apart from the constant disaffected rumours, they expressed their hostility by refusing to take part in any
celebration of sovereign power. During the summer, a
firework display given in the King's honour by the
Prince de Scubise was ruined by wind. Barbier commented: 'These reverses are beyond the power and
money of men.' Possibly he was indulging in his customary moralizing and deploring the vanity of such an
ostentatious display of wealth. On 26 August, the
Dauphine gave birth to 'a mere girl'. 'The cannons were
fired at Les Invalides and the Hôtel de Ville and at 7.30
the Hôtel de Ville was illuminated, but there were no
signs of pleasure or rejoicing in Paris.' Four days later
another celebration was held. D'Argenson tells that:

A man arrived from Versailles who said that there was
great anger at the people's miserable reaction to the
fireworks and illuminations held in honour of Monsieur
le Dauphin's daughter, the princess. He said that it had
been hard to tell whether there had been any spectators
at all, they had been so silent. The people were disen-
chanted with their master. Nothing could be more
deplorable.[29]

The mood of the people was cold and sad. Their
frosty reaction was nothing to do this time with the
outrageous expense of royal festivities but indicated
rather that the ceremonies which normally served as a
meeting point between King and people were no longer
effective. They were no longer prepared to play that

particular game. The festivities and the people's cold reception were not trivial matters. The populace were rejecting a gift from their sovereign thereby implying that relations between them were no longer possible.

Another year passed. Once again, in September 1751, a child was the catalyst of mutual estrangement. This time the Dauphine gave birth to a boy. The birth of an heir was a very important event manifesting the vitality of the monarchy and guaranteeing the permanence of royalty. But the magic had been irremediably broken:

> I have been assured that the people are filled with dismay rather than joy at the celebrations for the birth of the duc de Bourgogne. The order went out to close the shops for three days, but nobody paid any attention. There have never been so many fines imposed on people for failing to illuminate their houses. When the King passed by on his way to Notre Dame there were only a few hired rascals crying, 'Long live the King'. Consequently the King did not proceed to the Hôtel de Ville as he had promised.[30]

In 1866, Michelet wrote:

> The people's hearts were heavy. The storm clouds were gathering. Although it was the month of May, there was a cold, dry wind from the north. Serious turmoil was in the air. When the news spread that Berryer had gone to Versailles, the crowd went to the courts to wait for him. Some of the more impatient started crying, 'To Versailles!', others, 'Let us burn Versailles!' The tension was mounting.
>
> At Court, there was terror. At first nothing was said, then they said, 'It's nothing'. At that 'La Pompadour' set off to visit her daughter and dine with a friend in

Paris. Pale, her friend, told her, 'But, madame! Do not dine here. You will be torn to pieces.' She fled; she took wing and came sickly back to Versailles. All there were paralysed with fear.

On 23 May, matters grew far worse. Protected as they were by the Household Guards and the whole army, they still trembled. Guards were posted at the Pont de Sèvres and the Meudon pass.

One would have said the Bastille had already been taken and that the October 6 hunger marchers were on the move. Versailles was in panic. The women clung to the King, entwined themselves about him. He must not make the journey to Compiègne. Let him stay with his soldiers, safely surrounded by his Household Guard. They obtained their wish; he would not go. Then, a change of mind. The decision was pathetic – to make the journey, but in secret. That evening he slept at La Muette, then skirted the edges of Paris before dawn and broke away as though in flight. He said bitterly, 'Why should I look on a people who call me Herod?' In Paris they were saying, 'Is it disdain? It is fear.' Thus everything became embittered, and the rupture was complete.[31]

This is a fine passage but fallacious as are all prophecies made with hindsight. The visionary wants at all costs to see the 1750 riots as a rehearsal for the French Revolution. This is a mistake. If anything, it is the events of 1789 which were looking back to the turmoil of the past. The 1750 uprising was not looking to the future but was a heroic, albeit anachronistic spasm of protest against the state's ever increasing grip on people's daily lives. Fear was certainly unleashed, which doubtless also affected the court but, despite what d'Argenson believed, this was no radical new departure.

The revolt was a continued expression of old, familiar, though inverted, political ideals: that the ties binding a king to his people must be ties of love and fidelity. Michelet was mistaken, but not entirely. The affair of the child abductions was one tiny episode in the whole narrative of the eighteenth century, but it marked a significant shift of perspective, which began only then to be recognized. The violence and terror brought forth a new and awesome truth: 'The people no longer loved their kings whom once they had held so dear.'

Notes

Introduction

1 *Gazette d'Utrecht*, 2 June 1750.
2 L.-S. Mercier, *Tableau de Paris* (Amsterdam, 1782), vol. 1, pp. 32–3. Eng. tr. by W. and E. Jackson, *The Picture of Paris before and after the Revolution* (Routledge, London, 1929).
3 A.-P. Herlaut, 'Les enlèvements d'enfants à Paris en 1720 et 1750', *Revue historique*, t. CXXXIX, 1922, pp. 43–61 (which is still a fundamental source); Ch. Romon, 'L'affaire des enlèvements d'enfants dans les archives du Châtelet (1749–1750)', *Revue historique*, 3, 1983, pp. 55–95; J. Nicolas, 'La rumeur de Paris: rapts d'enfants en 1750', *L'Histoire*, no. 40, 1981, pp. 48–57; P. Piasenza, 'Rapimenti, polizia e rivolta: un conflitto sull'ordine pubblico a Parigi nel 1750', *Quaderni storici*, 64, 1987, pp. 129–51. We ourselves have published a very incomplete first version of this work under the title: 'Les règles de l'émeute: l'affaire des enlèvements d'enfants (Paris, mai 1750)', in *Mouvements populaires et conscience sociale, XVI–XIX siècle*, editor: J. Nicolas (Paris, 1985), pp. 635–46.

133

Chapter 1   The Landscape of Revolt

1 A. N., X2B 1367, 7 March 1750.
2 *Archers*: this was the term used during the Ancien Régime for the foot-soldiers whose task was to carry out the orders of the Lieutenant General in charge of Police. Their work was frequently to control the poor and particularly to round up vagrants to the 'Hôpitaux Généraux', which were the workhouses existing in all large towns in France.
3 Moreover, Christian Romon notes that almost half the revolts logged between 1711 and 1766 in the Châtelet archives happened between 1747 and 1751. See Ch. Romon, 'L'Affaire des enlèvements d'enfants'.
4 *Gardes françaises*: This was an infantry regiment, founded in 1563; no foreign national was allowed to join it. The *gardes françaises* was an élite regiment and formed part of the military establishment of the Royal Household although it was based in Paris rather than in Versailles. In 1789 the *gardes françaises* was to side with the revolutionaries in the capture of the Bastille, and was shortly afterwards disbanded by Louis XVI.
5 *Chronique de la Régence et du règne de Louis XV ou Journal de Barbier*, henceforward referred to as *Journal* (Paris, 1857), t. IV, p. 422.
6 A. N., AD III 7, Prosecutor Gueulette's notes.
7 B. N., mss Joly de Fleury, 1101, fo. 248.
8 Jacques-Louis Ménétra, *Journal de ma vie*, editor: D. Roche (Paris, 1982), p. 34.
9 A. N., AD III 7, Gueulette's notes.
10 A. N., X2B 1367.

11 A. N., Y 13 756, Commissioner de la Vergée's statement.

12 Duc de Luynes, *Mémoires sur la Cour de Louis XV (1735–1758)*, t. X (Paris, 1862), p. 266.

13 D'Argenson, *Journal et Mémoires*, editor: Rathery, t. VI (Paris, 1864), p. 202 onwards *Journal and Memoirs of the Marquis d'Argenson published from the manuscript*, E. J. B. Rathery, 1902; Barbier, *Journal*, t. IV, p. 427 onwards; Eng tr. Collé, *Journal et Mémoires*, editor: Bonhomme (Paris, 1868), t. I, p. 170.

14 B. N., mss Joly de Fleury, 1101, fo. 215, report of Fontaine, sergeant of the Guard; A. N., X2B 1368, interrogation of P. Defens.

15 B. Arsenal, Arch. Bastille, 10137, Inspector Roussel's register, 23 May 1750.

16 *Parlement*: the French *parlement* has been translated as 'parliament' throughout in the interest of the over-all text, but the two institutions were quite different. France had twelve *parlements* of which the one in Paris was by far the most important, having juris-diction over a third of the country. They were primarily law courts but also had extensive police powers. By the eighteenth century, membership of the *parlements* was venal and hereditary. Their political power was limited and the King had the ultimate power to enforce his authority on them.

17 Text in A. N., AD III 7.

18 The bulk of the information is gathered in the national archives under the classifications X2B 1367 and 1368 and in the Bibliothèque Nationale in the Joly de Fleury collection, mss 1101–1102, where the police and inquiry notes are filed.

19 The fullest account of the revolt is still that given by A.-P. Herlaut, drawing on the interrogations led by Councillor Severt, 'Les enlèvements d'enfants'; Ch. Romon, 'L'affaire des enlèvements d'enfants' adds some very useful detail, as does Paolo Piasenza whom we thank for having allowed us to see a forthcoming work. Map of the Paris riots in Romon, p. 68.

20 A. N., X2B 1367, interrogation of Adrienne Boucher, 8 June 1750.

21 A. N., X2B 1367, interrogation of Claude-Joseph Frizon, 18 July 1750.

22 A. N., X2B 1367, interrogation of Joseph Jacquet, 9 July 1750.

23 A. N., X2B 1367, interrogation of Marie-Françoise Lecomte, 8 June 1750.

24 For gossip sheets, see F. Moureau's definitions in *Le Journalisme d'Ancien Régime. Questions et propositions*, editor: P. Retat (Lyon, 1982), pp. 21–5.

25 D'Argenson, *Journal et Mémoires*, t. VI, pp. 101, 208, 205, 206, 211.

26 Ibid., p. 464.

27 Ibid., pp. 202, 204, 207, 216.

28 Ch. Aubertin, *L'Esprit public au XVIIIème siècle. Etude sur les mémoires et les correspondances politiques des contemporains (1715 à 1789)* (Paris, 1873), pp. 171–92.

29 Barbier, *Journal*, t. IV, pp. 401, 403, 422, 424, 432, 435.

30 One is reminded, for instance, of the Damiens affair, which was the subject of recent collected works edited by P. Retat, *L'Attentat de Damiens. Discours sur l'événement au XVIIIème siècle* (Lyons, 1979).

Chapter 2   Order in the City

1 A. Zysberg, *Les Galériens. Vies et destins de 60,000 forçats sur les galères de France, 1680–1748* (Paris, 1987), p. 72–5. On the politics of groups with regard to beggars, cf. Ch. Romon, 'Mendiants et policiers à Paris au XVIIIème siècle', *Histoire, économie et société*, 2, 1982, pp. 259–95.

2 B. N., mss Fds fr., N. A. 9328; and M. Giraud, *Histoire la Louisiane française* (Paris, 1966), t. III, pp. 252–76.

3 A. N., U 363, Delisle collection. Secret council of Parliament, 1687–1774.

4 D'Argenson, *Journal et Mémoires*, t. VI, p. 80, 30 November 1749.

5 Moufle d'Angerville, *Vie privée de Louis XV, ou Principaux Evénements, particularités et anecdotes de son règne* (London, 1781), t. II, p. 421–2. Eng. tr. by J. O. Justamond, *The Private Life of Lewis XV* (London, 1781).

6 A. N., X2B 1367, interrogations of Brucelle, Faillon, Le Blanc, Danguisy, Hamart.

7 A. Farge and M. Foucault, *Le Désordre des familles. Lettres de cachet des Archives de la Bastille* (Gallimard, Paris, 1982).

8 A. N., AD III 7, Prosecutor Gueulette's manuscript notes.

9 B. Arsenal, Arch. Bastille, 10137, Inspector Roussel's register, 23 May 1750.

10 Ibid., 26 May 1750, Inspector Poussot's observations.

11 A. N., X2B 1367, interrogations of P. Tournier and N. Passerat, 7 July 1750.

12 B. Arsenal, Arch. Bastille, 10140, Inspector Poussot's register, 1738–1754.

13 A. N., X2B 1367, interrogation of Antoine Severt, known as 'Parisien', 9 June 1750.

14 B. Arsenal, Arch. Bastille, 11732.

15 A. N., X2B 1367, interrogation of Sébastien Le Blanc, 31 May 1750; the information is confirmed by Jean-Auguste Hamart, a short-robed constable, ibid., 5 June 1750; also by Inspector Brucelle, ibid., 3 July 1750.

16 See P. Piasenza's excellent analysis in 'Rapimenti, polizia e rivolta' *Quaderni storici*. However, we are less convinced than the author of the 'normal' nature of police practices in 1750. For a general study of the Parisian police, see A. Williams, *The Police of Paris, 1717–1789* (Bâton Rouge, London, 1979).

17 Ch. Romon, 'L'affaire des enlèvements d'enfants'.

Chapter 3   *The Rules of Rebellion*

1 Barbier, *Journal*, t. IV, pp. 432–3.

2 See S. Moscovici, *L'Age des foules. Un traité historique de psychologie des masses* (Paris, 1981); and S. Barrows, *Distorting Mirrors, Visions of the Crowd in Late 19th Century France* (New Haven, London, 1981).

3 See G. Rudé's great work *The Crowd in the French Revolution* (Oxford, 1959). Fr. tr., with preface by G. Lefebvre (Paris, 1982).

4 E. P. Thompson, 'The moral economy of the English crowd in the 18th century', *Past and Present*, 50, 1971, pp. 76–136. See also N. Zemon Davis, 'The rites of violence', in *Society and Culture in Early*

Modern France (Stanford, 1975), pp. 152–87; also 'The sacred and the body social in 16th century Lyon', *Past and Present*, 90, 1981, pp. 40–70.

5 B. Arsenal, Arch. Bastille, 10137, Inspector Roussel's register.

6 B. N., mss Joly de Fleury, 1101; A. N., X2B 1367.

7 See, for instance, Frizon's evidence, A. N. X2B 1367, 18 July 1750; also that of the surveyor Langlois, B. N., mss Joly de Fleury, 1101, 23 May 1750.

8 On the meeting of two distinct styles at the heart of the uprising, a 'bourgeois style' and a 'popular style', see P. Piasenza's developments to appear in a forthcoming work on the organization of the Parisian police in the 17th and 18th centuries.

9 B. N., mss Joly de Fleury, 1101, 23 May 1750.

10 B. N., mss Joly de Fleury, 1102, Commissioner Defacq's statement, 22 May 1750.

11 A. N., X2B 1368, interrogation of Geneviève Olivier, 31 May 1750.

12 The best description of the building is that of Louis Devaux, A. N., X2B 1367, 5 June 1750.

13 For this passage we have used the interrogations of Louis Devaux and Marie-Françoise Lecomte, A. N., X2B 1367, 5 and 8 June 1750, also that of Geneviève Olivier, A. N., X2B 1368, 31 May 1750.

14 A. N., X2B 1368, interrogation of Louis Paillard, 20 June 1750.

15 A. N., Y 13756, Commissioner de la Vergée's statement. The clerk Paillard reports that 'The witness said that he would administer justice . . . .'.

16 A. N., Y 11932, cited by Ch. Romon, 'L'affaire des enlèvements d'enfants', p. 67.

17 Barbier, *Journal*, t. IV, p. 435.
18 This episode is traced in the long interrogation of the clerk Louis Paillard, op. cit.
19 A. N., X2B 1367, interrogation of Claude-Toussaint Parisis 10 July 1750. It is also confirmed from the evidence of Paillard, op. cit.
20 Prosecutor Gueulette, A. N., AD III 7, May 1750.
21 D'Argenson, *Journal*, t. VI, pp. 209–10.

Chapter 4   Truth and Rumour

1 Discussion in Ch. Romon, 'L'affaire des enlève-ments d'enfants', pp. 87–8. But the very definition of 'wounded' is imprecise in the texts.
2 A. N., X2B 1367, Louis Taconnet's statement, 29 May 1750.
3 B. N., mss Joly de Fleury, 1101, evidence of Jean-François Joly, 25 June 1750.
4 A. N., X2B 1367, Marguerite Ollier's statement, 2 June 1750.
5 A. N., X2B 1367, interrogation of Sébastien Le Blanc, 31 May 1750; interrogation of Julien Dan-guisy, 5 and 16 June 1750; interrogation of Jean-Auguste Hamart, 5 June 1750; interrogation of Joseph Faillon, 13 June 1750; interrogation of Jac-ques Brucelle, 3 July 1750. Extracts from Le Blanc's diary listing his arrests are appended to his interro-gation.
6 The episode is related in three concurring statements: that of Jean-Baptiste Feuchère, acolyte charged with the instruction of the poor children of the parish of Saint-Gervais, A. N., X2B 1367, 27 May

1750; also those of François Copin and his mother, Marguerite Lebel, ibid., 29 May 1750. This is the only example where the abduction of girls is mentioned, but the precision of the statements leaves no doubt about the truth of the episode.

7 A. N., X2B 1368, René Gayard's statement, 13 June 1750.

8 A. N., X2B 1367, Joseph Peyssaud's statement, 22 June 1750.

9 A. N., X2B 1368, Pierre-François Dumont's statement, 13 June 1750.

10 A. N., X2B 1367, Joseph Faillon's statement, 13 June 1750.

11 On this point, see P. Piasenza, 'Rapimenti, polizia e rivolta'. See also the evidence of Mercier who was witness to one of these scenes: 'A calm witness told me unemotionally: "Leave it, sir, it is nothing, it is a police abduction." ' (*Tableau de Paris*, II, XLVII.)

12 Herlaut, 'Les enlèvements d'enfants', pp. 43–9.

13 A. N., X2B 1368, statement of Jacques Descoings, cavalryman of the *maréchaussée*, 20 June 1750; see also B. N., mss Joly de Fleury, 1102, fos 128–9 (anonymous denunciation); D'Argenson, *Journal*, t. VI, p. 207.

14 B. M. Orléans, Fonds Lenoir, ms 1422, fos 302–4.

15 D. Garrioch, *Neighbourhood and Community in Paris, 1740–1790* (Cambridge, 1986); also D. Roche, *Le Peuple de Paris* (Paris, 1979), pp. 255–6.

16 A. N., X2B 1367, statements of J.-B. Feuchère, 27 May 1750; Marie Guérin, widow Geoffroy, 27 May 1750; Marie-Louise Pigeon, 27 May 1750; Gabriel Didier, 29 May 1750.

17 A. N., X2B 1368, M.-J. Fouquet's statement, 22 June 1750.

18 B. N., mss Joly de Fleury, 1101, fo. 227. For a study of the way in which rumour manipulates known facts into a plausible tale, see Steven L. Kaplan's analysis *Le complot de famine: histoire d'une rumeur au XVIIIème siècle* (Paris, 1982).

19 B. Arsenal, Arch. Bastille, 10136, 22 and 23 May 1750.

20 Moufle d'Angerville, *Vie privée de Louis XV*, II, p. 420.

21 See, for example, A. N., X2B 1367, 27 May 1750; ibid., Anne-France Cornet's statement; ibid., M.-M. Bizet's statement, 29 May 1750; ibid., F. Linotte's statement, 13 June 1750; ibid., M. Duperrier's statement, 2 June 1750.

22 A. N., X2B 1368, F. Linotte's statement, 13 June 1750; see also the case of the Laporte child, X2B 1367, 27 May 1750; ibid., M.-M. Bizet's statement, 29 May 1750.

23 Barbier, *Journal*, t. II, p. 37; t. IV, pp. 356–8, 404–5, 407–10, 441, 448–9.

24 Barbier, *Journal*, t. IV, p. 423; d'Argenson, *Mémoires*, Bibliothèque Elzévirienne (Paris, 1857), p. 331. (The passage was removed in Rathery's edition); *Correspondance de la marquise de Pompadour*, editor: Malassis (Paris, 1878), p. 55. Eng. tr. *Letters of the Marchioness of Pompadour from MDCCXLVI to MDCCLI* (T. Codell, London, 1772); Ménétra, *Journal de ma vie*, p. 34.

25 Mercier, 'Tableau de Paris', II, XLVII; Moufle d'Angerville, *Vie privée de Louis XV*, II, p. 421; B. M. Orléans, Fonds Lenoir, ms 1422, fo. 304; J.

Peuchet, *Mémoires tirées des archives de la police* (Paris, 1838), t. II, p. 127.

26 B. N., mss Joly de Fleury, 280, fo. 310; Peuchet, *Mémoires*, t. II, p. 136; On the Lyons affair, see M. Garden, *Lyon et les Lyonnais au XVIIIème siècle* (Paris, 1970), p. 585–6, a work which draws on Morel de Valeire, 'Petite chronique lyonnaise, 30 décembre 1768', *Revue du Lyonnais*, II, 1851, p. 276; there is a file of archives in A. D. Rhône, C6 (28 November 1768) which Marcel Gauchet was kind enough to indicate to us but which we discovered too late to be able to use; on the Mantes affair, see Ravaisson, 'Archives de la Bastille' (1762) vol. 18, p. 205.

27 Christopher Hill, to whom we submitted this hypothesis, assured us that he had never come across it in English seventeenth-century pamphlet literature.

28 B. Arsenal, Arch. Bastille, 10137, Inspector Roussel's register, 22 May 1750; D'Argenson, *Journal*, t. VI, p. 219.

29 Bibliothèque de Port-Royal, Le Paige collection, no. 515, fo. 147 (letter to Madame Le Paige, 25 May 1750). We would like to thank Catherine Maire to whom we are indebted for this source.

30 See Saul N. Brady, *The Disease of the Soul. Leprosy in Medieval Literature* (Ithaca, London, 1974); also Geneviève Pichon's unpublished thesis, 'La représentation médiévale de la lèpre', University of Paris III, 2 vols (Paris, 1979).

31 G. Daniel, *Histoire de France depuis l'établissement de la monarchie française dans les Gaules* (1755 edition), t. VII, p. 640. Eng. tr. by G. Strahan, *The History of France from the time the French monarchy was estab-*

lished in Gaul to the death of Louis XIV, 5 vols (London, 1726). Voltaire criticized Daniel's work but he drew a lot of material from it for the *Essai sur les moeurs*, which he was working on during the 1750s (chapter XCVI). However, there is no mention of the affair in the *Correspondance*, nor in the *Précis du siécle de Louis XV* (1768).

32 See, for example, the description of the illness offered by the doctor Théodoric de Cervia in the thirteenth century to be found in Brody, *The Disease of the Soul*, pp. 35–7.

33 J. and W. Grimm, *Der arme Heinrich von Hartmann von Aue, herausgegeben und erklärt* (Berlin, 1815); see also P. Cassel, *Die Symbolik des Blutes und "Der arme Heinrich" von Hartmann von Aue* (Berlin, 1882).

Chapter 5   The Unloved

1 D'Argenson, *Journal*, t. VI, p. 239.

2 A. N., X2B 1367, interrogations of Charles-François Urbain, 29 May, 11 June and 15 July 1750.

3 A. N., X2B 1368, Marie-Charlotte Duval's statement, 20 June 1750.

4 A. N., X2B 1367, interrogations of J.-B. Charvat, 22 July 1750 and J.-B. Lebeau, 14 July 1750.

5 Barbier, *Journal*, t. IV, p. 445.

6 Ibid., p. 456.

7 They were to unite again in September, this time in one solid body; see D'Argenson, *Journal*, t. VI, p. 259.

8 B. Arsenal, Arch. Bastille, Gazetins de la police secrète, 10158, September 1728.

9 Ibid., September and November 1728.

10 Ibid., August 1728.

11 Arch. Bastille, Gazetins, 10159, August 1729.

12 Arch. Bastille, Gazetins, 10161, 8 February 1732.

13 See D. Van Kley, *The Damiens Affair and the Unraveling of the Ancien Régime, 1750–1770* (Princeton, 1984), pp. 226–65.

14 Arch. Bastille, Gazetins, 10159, 3 March 1729.

15 S. L. Kaplan, *Le complot de famine*.

16 Barbier, *Journal*, t. IV, p. 377.

17 *Nouvelles Ecclésiastiques*: an underground publication printed by the Jansenists.

18 B. Arsenal, MS 6889. See also D'Argenson, *Journal*, t. VI, p. 172: 'Recently, several of the convulsionaries known as "secouristes" have been interrogated: several of them admitted to wanting the death of the King, which causes fear' (17 March 1750).

19 D'Argenson, *Journal*, t. VI, p. 15.

20 The theme is developed by J. Sgard in an unpublished work which he was kind enough to send us; his forthcoming work is 'Naissance de l'opinion publique'.

21 Arch. Bastille, 10029, Journal of the chevalier de Mouchy (1745–1749).

22 D'Argenson, *Journal*, t. VI, p. 152.

23 A. N., X2B 1368, information given by Marguerite Benoist, undated.

24 Arch. Bastille, 10137, Inspector Roussel's register, 26 May 1750.

25 A. N., X2B 1367, interrogation of Antoine Severt, known as 'Parisien', 9 June 1750.

26 D'Argenson, *Journal*, t. VI, p. 135.

27 Van Kley, *The Damiens affair*, pp. 37–8.

28 Barbier, *Journal*, t. IV, p. 440; D'Argenson, *Journal,* t. VI, p. 218. See also the *Correspondance de la marquise de Pompadour*, p. 59 (15 June 1750).

29 Barbier, *Journal*, t. IV, pp. 465–6; D'Argenson, *Journal,* t. VI, pp. 250–1.

30 D'Argenson, *Journal*, t. VI, p. 474.

31 Michelet, *Histoire de France*, XVI (Paris, 1866), pp. 287–8. Eng. tr. by W. K. Kelly, *History of France*, 2 vols (London 1844–46); and by G. H. Smith, *History of France*, 2 vols (London 1844–47).